www.prim-ed.com

CW01066529

INCLUDES
DIGITAL CONTENT

PRIMARY
MATHS

2014 CURRICULUM

Resources and teacher ideas for every objective of the 2014 curriculum

Number

- Number and place value
- Addition and subtraction
- Multiplication and division
- Fractions

WRITTEN BY
TEACHERS FOR TEACHERS

6128

Published by Prim-Ed Publishing 2014
Copyright© Clare Way 2004
ISBN 978-1-84654-760-7
PR–6128

Titles available in this series:

6124	Primary Maths	Year 1, Book 1 – Number
6125	Primary Maths	Year 1, Book 2 – Measurement and Geometry
6126	Primary Maths	Year 2, Book 1 – Number
6127	Primary Maths	Year 2, Book 2 – Measurement, Geometry and Statistics
6128	Primary Maths	Year 3, Book 1 – Number
6129	Primary Maths	Year 3, Book 2 – Measurement, Geometry and Statistics
6130	Primary Maths	Year 4, Book 1 – Number
6131	Primary Maths	Year 4, Book 2 – Measurement, Geometry and Statistics
6132	Primary Maths	Year 5, Book 1 – Number
6133	Primary Maths	Year 5, Book 2 – Measurement, Geometry and Statistics
6134	Primary Maths	Year 6, Book 1 – Number, Algebra, Ratio and Proportion
6135	Primary Maths	Year 6, Book 2 – Measurement, Geometry and Statistics

Internet websites

In some cases, websites or specific URLs may be recommended. While these are checked and rechecked at the time of publication, the publisher has no control over any subsequent changes which may be made to webpages. It is *strongly* recommended that the class teacher checks *all* URLs before allowing pupils to access them.

View all pages online

Foreword

Primary Maths is a photocopiable, six-level, year-specific series designed to address the Primary National Curriculum for Mathematics objectives of:
- number
- measurement
- geometry
- statistics.

Each book in the Primary Maths series includes:
- at least one activity page for each objective which can be photocopied or displayed on an interactive whiteboard
- comprehensive teachers notes to accompany each activity
- additional teachers notes on activities and games
- assessment checklists
- additional photocopiable resources
- interactive whiteboard resources to download.

The Year 3 books in the Primary Maths series are:

Primary Maths – Number

Primary Maths – Measurement, Geometry and Statistics

Contents

Teachers notes

How to use this book

The **Primary Maths** series provides teachers with a number of varied and challenging activities. At least one activity, often more, is provided for each objective of the **Primary National Curriculum for Mathematics**.

Suggestions for using the activities in this book:

Objective:

- *Decide which curriculum objective you wish to address and choose the appropriate activity page(s).*

Oral work and mental calculation starter:

- *Choose which oral and mental activities you will use, from the list provided, to introduce the lesson or sharpen pupils' skills.*

- *Some of the activities have accompanying interactive whiteboard activities to help introduce the lesson and capture pupils' attention.*

- *These activities should occupy the first 5–10 minutes of the lesson.*

Main teaching activity:

- *Decide how much teacher input you will provide for the main activity and whether pupils will be working individually, in pairs or as a group.*

- *Depending upon the abilities of the pupils in your class, decide whether any additional activities will be needed, from the list provided, or whether these can be used during subsequent lessons.*

- *This activity should occupy approximately 40 minutes.*

Plenary:

- *Decide what opportunities will be provided during the plenary session. Will pupils be given the opportunity to share and explain work, compare strategies used or summarise the key facts they have learnt?*

- *Think about how you can use the plenary session to assess pupils' progress and therefore inform your future planning.*

- *The plenary should occupy the final 15 minutes of the lesson.*

Pupil activity pages:

The pupil activities follow a common format:

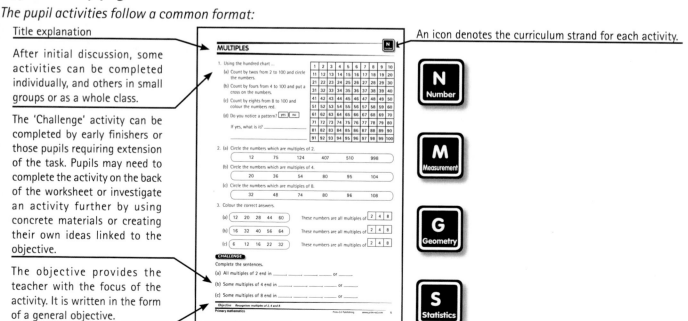

Title explanation

After initial discussion, some activities can be completed individually, and others in small groups or as a whole class.

The 'Challenge' activity can be completed by early finishers or those pupils requiring extension of the task. Pupils may need to complete the activity on the back of the worksheet or investigate an activity further by using concrete materials or creating their own ideas linked to the objective.

The objective provides the teacher with the focus of the activity. It is written in the form of a general objective.

An icon denotes the curriculum strand for each activity.

Teachers notes

How to use this book

Teachers pages

A teachers page accompanies each pupil worksheet. It provides the following information:

The **objective** tells the teacher which strand and objective from the **Primary National Curriculum for Mathematics** is being covered.

Oral work and mental calculation activities are suggested, for introducing the lesson or sharpening/developing oral and mental skills. The activities should occupy the first 10 minutes of the lesson.

Some activities have **interactive whiteboard** activities available to download. If an interactive activity is provided it is listed here.

The title of the **main teaching activity** is given. The photocopiable activity is on the page facing the teachers notes. The main activity should occupy approximately 40 minutes.

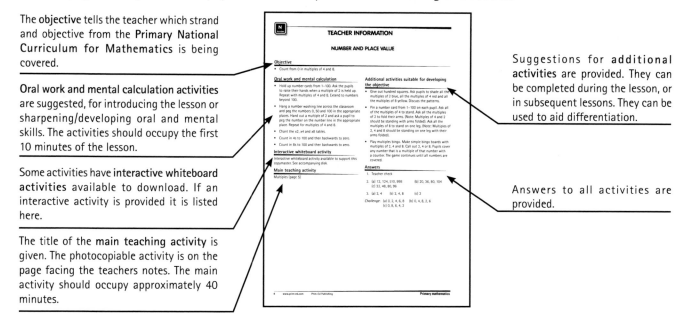

Suggestions for **additional activities** are provided. They can be completed during the lesson, or in subsequent lessons. They can be used to aid differentiation.

Answers to all activities are provided.

Assessment

Assessment checklists have been included for the Year 3 'Number' objectives. See pages viii–x. These can be used to assess each pupil's understanding of the key objectives covered.

Use the key to write the appropriate code next to each task the pupil completes.

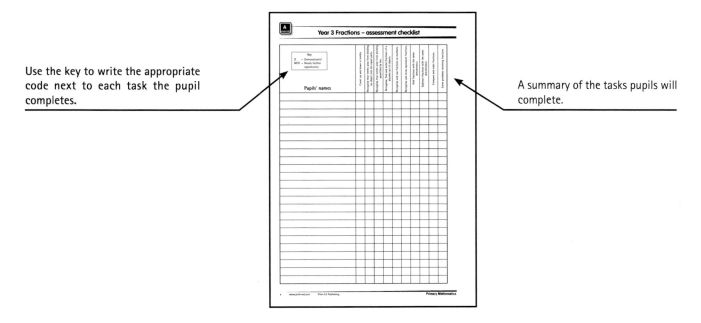

A summary of the tasks pupils will complete.

- *Teaching notes for the 'Number' strands have been included on page vii. These comprise background information and suggested activities and games.*

- *Extra teacher resources have been included on pages xi–xiv. These can be enlarged if necessary and used in appropriate activities or as display posters.*

- *Interactive whiteboard activities have been provided to help teach the objectives. These can be downloaded from www.prim-ed.com.*

Teachers notes

Setting up a mathematics classroom

By having the following materials and visual representations around them, pupils can better engage in mathematical learning.

- *Allow room to move so pupils can investigate things around the room. Organise desks and floor space appropriately.*

- *Display a 'Numbers' chart.*

- *Display a number line at a level where pupils can use it.*

- *Display numbers, number words and a visual representation of numbers.*

- *Display addition and subtraction facts.*

- *Display a 100 square.*

- *Ensure you have a good range of maths games and use them regularly.*

- *Display 'times tables' charts.*

- *Have an analogue and digital clock in the classroom.*

- *Display pictures of labelled 2-D and 3-D shapes.*

- *Provide construction materials such as cardboard boxes, cylinders, paper, scissors and so on.*

- *Ensure you have adequate concrete materials to teach each strand (refer to page vii).*

- *Allow pupils opportunities to investigate outside the classroom in the school environment.*

- *Display a chart showing simple equivalent fractions.*

- *Display or make various graphs such as pictograms, bar charts, block graphs, Venn diagrams and Carroll diagrams.*

- *Display a class birthday chart which includes the months of the year.*

- *Display and use a calendar.*

- *Have computer software related to mathematics available for use on the classroom computer(s) or in the computer room.*

- *Display a poster showing all coins and notes.*

- *Provide a range of measuring equipment for length, mass and capacity.*

- *Display the four compass directions: north, south, east and west.*

- *Ensure you have a good selection of interactive maths resources for use on a whiteboard (refer to website for downloads – www.prim-ed.com).*

Teachers notes

Activities and games

- Play 'Bingo' to consolidate basic facts etc. Vary by calling out the answer in some games and the number sentence or problem in others. Blank bingo cards are on page xix.

4 x 4	12 + 2	3 x 5
10 – 4	20 – 1	6 x 3

16

5 x 6

15	8	21
7	30	16

- Divide the class into teams and select one pupil from each team to stand at the board ready to write. Call out a number (e.g. 1089) or basic fact (e.g. 25 – 6, 7 x 5, double 12). The first pupil to write the correct answer wins a point for his/her team.

- Use Base 10 place value blocks to show the difference between two sets of numbers, either by direct comparison of the two sets or by taking the smaller away from the larger number.

- Set up a class 'shop'. Pupils can purchase goods using coins and notes. Pupils take turns to act as the shopkeeper and give the correct change.

- Pupils exchange teacher-distributed coins for notes and notes for coins. Initially, pupils work from a central 'bank'. This activity also works as a reward system with pupils earning money tokens for good work, good behaviour and so on.

- Use real life situations and ask pupils to state the operation needed to solve the given word problem; for example, 'There are 25 pupils in our class, and I have 125 jellybeans. How many jellybeans will each pupil get?' (5 jellybeans)

- Look for number patterns in all areas of mathematics, as well as in daily routines, at school, at home or in the wider community.

Materials required

- place value blocks
- place value mats (page xii)
- fraction charts (see pages xvii and xviii)
- 100s chart (see page xiii)
- number lines
- bingo cards (see page xix)

- interconnecting cubes
- abacus
- tables charts (see pages xv–xvi)
- number word flashcards (see page xi)

Year 3 Number and place value – assessment checklist

Pupils' names	Count from 0 in multiples of 4 and 8.	Count from 0 in multiples of 50 and 100.	Find 10 or 100 more than a given number.	Find 10 or 100 less than a given number.	Recognise the place value of each digit in a three-digit number.	Compare and order numbers up to 1000.	Identify, represent and estimate numbers using different representations.	Read and write numbers up to 1000 in numerals and in words.	Solve number and practical problems.

Key
D = Demonstrated
NFO = Needs further opportunity

Year 3 Addition, subtraction, multiplication and division – assessment checklist

A Assessment

Key
D = Demonstrated
NFO = Needs further opportunity

Pupils' names	Add numbers mentally (HTU + HTU/TU/U).	Subtract numbers mentally (HTU – HTU/TU/U).	Add numbers with up to three digits, using formal written methods of columnar addition.	Subtract numbers with up to three digits, using formal written methods of columnar subtraction.	Estimate the answer to a calculation.	Use inverse operations to check answers.	Solve missing number problems.	Solve problems using number facts, place value and more complex addition and subtraction.	Recall and use multiplication facts for the 3, 4 and 8 multiplication tables.	Recall and use division facts for the 3, 4 and 8 multiplication tables.	Mentally calculate multiplication of two-digit numbers by one-digit numbers.	Mentally calculate division of two-digit numbers by one-digit numbers.	Use formal written methods to complete multiplication.	Use formal written methods to complete division.	Solve missing number problems.	Solve positive integer scaling problems.	Solve correspondence problems in which n objects are connected to m objects.

Year 3 Fractions – assessment checklist

Pupils' names	Count up and down in tenths.	Recognise that tenths arise from dividing an object into ten equal parts.	Recognise that tenths arise from dividing quantities by ten.	Recognise, find and write fractions of a discrete set of objects.	Recognise and use fractions as numbers.	Recognise and show equivalent fractions.	Add fractions with the same denominator.	Subtract fractions with the same denominator.	Compare and order fractions.	Solve problems involving fractions.

Key
D = Demonstrated
NFO = Needs further opportunity

Teacher resources

Number words

10	ten	200	two hundred
20	twenty	300	three hundred
30	thirty	400	four hundred
40	forty	500	five hundred
50	fifty	600	six hundred
60	sixty	700	seven hundred
70	seventy	800	eight hundred
80	eighty	900	nine hundred
90	ninety	1000	one thousand
100	one hundred		

Teacher resources

HTU

Hundreds	Tens	Ones

Teacher resources

100 chart

1	2	3	4	5	6	7	8	9	10
11	12	13	14	15	16	17	18	19	20
21	22	23	24	25	26	27	28	29	30
31	32	33	34	35	36	37	38	39	40
41	42	43	44	45	46	47	48	49	50
51	52	53	54	55	56	57	58	59	60
61	62	63	64	65	66	67	68	69	70
71	72	73	74	75	76	77	78	79	80
81	82	83	84	85	86	87	88	89	90
91	92	93	94	95	96	97	98	99	100

0–99 chart

0	1	2	3	4	5	6	7	8	9
10	11	12	13	14	15	16	17	18	19
20	21	22	23	24	25	26	27	28	29
30	31	32	33	34	35	36	37	38	39
40	41	42	43	44	45	46	47	48	49
50	51	52	53	54	55	56	57	58	59
60	61	62	63	64	65	66	67	68	69
70	71	72	73	74	75	76	77	78	79
80	81	82	83	84	85	86	87	88	89
90	91	92	93	94	95	96	97	98	99

Teacher resources

Basic multiplication facts

X	0	1	2	3	4	5	6	7	8	9	10
0	0	0	0	0	0	0	0	0	0	0	0
1	0	1	2	3	4	5	6	7	8	9	10
2	0	2	4	6	8	10	12	14	16	18	20
3	0	3	6	9	12	15	18	21	24	27	30
4	0	4	8	12	16	20	24	28	32	36	40
5	0	5	10	15	20	25	30	35	40	45	50
6	0	6	12	18	24	30	36	42	48	54	60
7	0	7	14	21	28	35	42	49	56	63	70
8	0	8	16	24	32	40	48	56	64	72	80
9	0	9	18	27	36	45	54	63	72	81	90
10	0	10	20	30	40	50	60	70	80	90	100

Basic multiplication facts

X	0	1	2	3	4	5	6	7	8	9	10
0	0	0	0	0	0	0	0	0	0	0	0
1	0	1	2	3	4	5	6	7	8	9	10
2	0	2	4	6	8	10	12	14	16	18	20
3	0	3	6	9	12	15	18	21	24	27	30
4	0	4	8	12	16	20	24	28	32	36	40
5	0	5	10	15	20	25	30	35	40	45	50
6	0	6	12	18	24	30	36	42	48	54	60
7	0	7	14	21	28	35	42	49	56	63	70
8	0	8	16	24	32	40	48	56	64	72	80
9	0	9	18	27	36	45	54	63	72	81	90
10	0	10	20	30	40	50	60	70	80	90	100

x 2, x 5 and x 10 tables

x 10

$1 \times 10 = 10$

$2 \times 10 = 20$

$3 \times 10 = 30$

$4 \times 10 = 40$

$5 \times 10 = 50$

$6 \times 10 = 60$

$7 \times 10 = 70$

$8 \times 10 = 80$

$9 \times 10 = 90$

$10 \times 10 = 100$

x 5

$1 \times 5 = 5$

$2 \times 5 = 10$

$3 \times 5 = 15$

$4 \times 5 = 20$

$5 \times 5 = 25$

$6 \times 5 = 30$

$7 \times 5 = 35$

$8 \times 5 = 40$

$9 \times 5 = 45$

$10 \times 5 = 50$

x 2

$1 \times 2 = 2$

$2 \times 2 = 4$

$3 \times 2 = 6$

$4 \times 2 = 8$

$5 \times 2 = 10$

$6 \times 2 = 12$

$7 \times 2 = 14$

$8 \times 2 = 16$

$9 \times 2 = 18$

$10 \times 2 = 20$

Teacher resources

x 3, x 4 and x 8 tables

x 3

$1 \times 3 = 3$
$2 \times 3 = 6$
$3 \times 3 = 9$
$4 \times 3 = 12$
$5 \times 3 = 15$
$6 \times 3 = 18$
$7 \times 3 = 21$
$8 \times 3 = 24$
$9 \times 3 = 27$
$10 \times 3 = 30$

x 4

$1 \times 4 = 4$
$2 \times 4 = 8$
$3 \times 4 = 12$
$4 \times 4 = 16$
$5 \times 4 = 20$
$6 \times 4 = 24$
$7 \times 4 = 28$
$8 \times 4 = 32$
$9 \times 4 = 36$
$10 \times 4 = 40$

x 8

$1 \times 8 = 8$
$2 \times 8 = 16$
$3 \times 8 = 24$
$4 \times 8 = 32$
$5 \times 8 = 40$
$6 \times 8 = 48$
$7 \times 8 = 56$
$8 \times 8 = 64$
$9 \times 8 = 72$
$10 \times 8 = 80$

Fractions

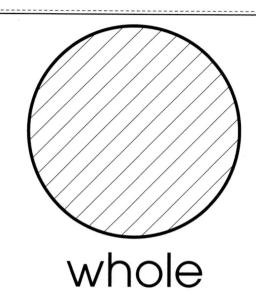

whole

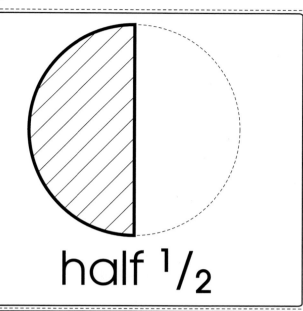

half $^1/_2$

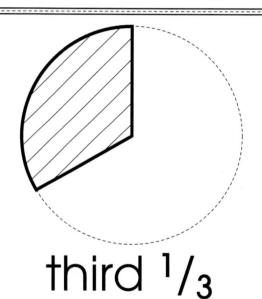

third $^1/_3$

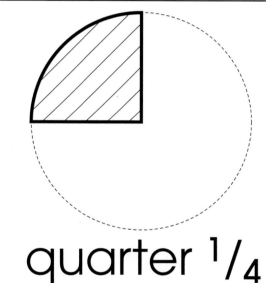

quarter $^1/_4$

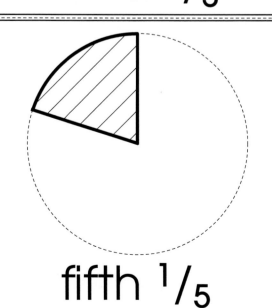

fifth $^1/_5$

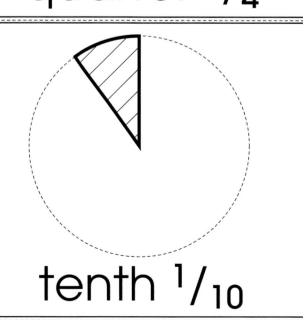

tenth $^1/_{10}$

Teacher resources

Equivalent fractions

whole $\frac{1}{1}$							
half				$\frac{1}{2}$			
quarter		$\frac{1}{4}$		$\frac{1}{4}$		$\frac{1}{4}$	
eighth	$\frac{1}{8}$	$\frac{1}{8}$	$\frac{1}{8}$	$\frac{1}{8}$	$\frac{1}{8}$	$\frac{1}{8}$	$\frac{1}{8}$

whole $\frac{1}{1}$									
half					$\frac{1}{2}$				
fifth		$\frac{1}{5}$		$\frac{1}{5}$		$\frac{1}{5}$		$\frac{1}{5}$	
tenth	$\frac{1}{10}$	$\frac{1}{10}$	$\frac{1}{10}$	$\frac{1}{10}$	$\frac{1}{10}$	$\frac{1}{10}$	$\frac{1}{10}$	$\frac{1}{10}$	$\frac{1}{10}$

Bingo cards (blank)

TEACHER INFORMATION

NUMBER AND PLACE VALUE

Objective

- Count from 0 in multiples of 4 and 8.

Oral work and mental calculation

- Count on as a class in 2s/4s/8s starting from a two-digit number. Extend to from a three-digit number.

- Count backwards in 2s/4s/8s, starting from a two-digit number. Extend to from a three-digit number.

- Use a class number board. Pick a pupil to choose a number to start from. Count from that number, forwards in 2s/4s/8s and then backwards in 2s/4s/8s.

Main teaching activity

Group counting (page 3)

Additional activities suitable for developing the objective

- Make a number line around the perimeter of the classroom or playground. Pupils stand on the number line and follow instructions; for example, 'walk forward 4'.

- Use a number line to respond to questions; for example,

  Count on 30 in threes from 27.

  Count back 20 in fours from 44.

  Count on in fives from 25 to 55. How many fives did you count?

- Complete number sequences; for example, 327, 330, 333, ___. Explain the sequences.

- Give each pupil a hundred square. Count by threes and draw a red circle around each answer. Count in fours and draw a blue triangle around each answer. Count in fives and colour the squares. Discuss any patterns.

Answers

1. Teacher check

2. Teacher check

3. Teacher check

4. (a) 30, 40, 50, 55, 70   (b) 36, 42, 51, 57, 60
   (c) 80, 60, 40, 30, 20   (d) 95, 80, 70, 55, 50
   (e) 33, 27, 18, 9, 3   (f) 72, 64, 56, 52, 40
   (g) 80, 64, 56, 40, 16, 8

Challenge: Teacher check

GROUP COUNTING

1	2	3	4	5	6	7	8	9	10
11	12	13	14	15	16	17	18	19	20
21	22	23	24	25	26	27	28	29	30
31	32	33	34	35	36	37	38	39	40
41	42	43	44	45	46	47	48	49	50
51	52	53	54	55	56	57	58	59	60
61	62	63	64	65	66	67	68	69	70
71	72	73	74	75	76	77	78	79	80
81	82	83	84	85	86	87	88	89	90
91	92	93	94	95	96	97	98	99	100

1. Count in 2s from 0 to 100. You may wish to use the hundreds chart to help you.

_____

_____

_____

_____

2. Count in 4s from 0 to 100.

_____

_____

3. Count in 8s from 0 to 96.

_____

_____

4. Fill in the missing numbers.

  (a) 20, 25, _____, 35, _____, 45, _____, _____, 60, 65, _____

  (b) 30, 33, _____, 39, _____, 45, 48, _____, 54, _____, _____

  (c) 100, 90, _____, 70, _____, 50, _____, _____, _____, 10, 0

  (d) _____, 90, 85, _____, 75, _____, 65, 60, _____, _____, 45

  (e) 36, _____, 30, _____, 24, 21, _____, 15, 12, _____, 6, _____, 0

  (f) 80, 76, _____, 68, _____, 60, _____, _____, 48, 44, _____

  (g) 96, 88, _____, 72, _____, _____, 48, _____, 32, 24, _____, _____, 0

CHALLENGE

On the back of the sheet, count backwards from 100 to 0.

Objective   *Counts forwards and backwards in 2s, 3s, 4s, 5s, 8s and 10s.*

TEACHER INFORMATION

NUMBER AND PLACE VALUE

Objective

- Count from 0 in multiples of 4 and 8.

Oral work and mental calculation

- Hold up number cards from 1–100. Ask the pupils to raise their hands when a multiple of 2 is held up. Repeat with multiples of 4 and 8. Extend to numbers beyond 100.

- Hang a number washing line across the classroom and peg the numbers 0, 50 and 100 in the appropriate places. Hand out a multiple of 2 and ask a pupil to peg the number on the number line in the appropriate place. Repeat for multiples of 4 and 8.

- Chant the x2, x4 and x8 tables.

- Count in 4s to 100 and then backwards to zero.

- Count in 8s to 100 and then backwards to zero.

Interactive whiteboard activity

Interactive whiteboard activity available to support this copymaster. Visit *www.prim-ed.com*.

Main teaching activity

Multiples (page 5)

Additional activities suitable for developing the objective

- Give out hundred squares. Ask pupils to shade all the multiples of 2 blue, all the multiples of 4 red and all the multiples of 8 yellow. Discuss the patterns.

- Pin a number card from 1–100 on each pupil. Ask all of the multiples of 4 to stand. Ask all the multiples of 2 to fold their arms. (Note: Multiples of 4 and 2 should be standing with arms folded). Ask all the multiples of 8 to stand on one leg. (Note: Multiples of 2, 4 and 8 should be standing on one leg with their arms folded).

- Play multiples bingo. Make simple bingo boards with multiples of 2, 4 and 8. Call out 2, 4 or 8. Pupils cover any number that is a multiple of that number with a counter. The game continues until all numbers are covered.

Answers

1. Teacher check

2. (a) 12, 124, 510, 998   (b) 20, 36, 80, 104
   (c) 32, 48, 80, 96

3. (a) 2, 4   (b) 2, 4, 8   (c) 2

Challenge: (a) 0, 2, 4, 6, 8   (b) 0, 4, 8, 2, 6
            (c) 0, 8, 6, 4, 2

MULTIPLES

1. Using the hundreds chart ...

   (a) Count in twos from 2 to 100 and circle the numbers.

   (b) Count in fours from 4 to 100 and put a cross on the numbers.

   (c) Count in eights from 8 to 100 and colour the numbers red.

   (d) Do you notice a pattern? ☐ yes ☐ no

   If yes, what is it? _____

   _____

1	2	3	4	5	6	7	8	9	10
11	12	13	14	15	16	17	18	19	20
21	22	23	24	25	26	27	28	29	30
31	32	33	34	35	36	37	38	39	40
41	42	43	44	45	46	47	48	49	50
51	52	53	54	55	56	57	58	59	60
61	62	63	64	65	66	67	68	69	70
71	72	73	74	75	76	77	78	79	80
81	82	83	84	85	86	87	88	89	90
91	92	93	94	95	96	97	98	99	100

2. (a) Circle the numbers which are multiples of 2.

   | 12 | 75 | 124 | 407 | 510 | 998 |

   (b) Circle the numbers which are multiples of 4.

   | 20 | 36 | 54 | 80 | 95 | 104 |

   (c) Circle the numbers which are multiples of 8.

   | 32 | 48 | 74 | 80 | 96 | 108 |

3. Colour the correct answers.

   (a) (12   20   28   44   60)   These numbers are all multiples of ☐ 2 ☐ 4 ☐ 8

   (b) (16   32   40   56   64)   These numbers are all multiples of ☐ 2 ☐ 4 ☐ 8

   (c) (6   12   16   22   32)   These numbers are all multiples of ☐ 2 ☐ 4 ☐ 8

CHALLENGE

Complete the sentences.

(a) All multiples of 2 end in _____, _____, _____, _____ or _____.

(b) Some multiples of 4 end in _____, _____, _____, _____ or _____.

(c) Some multiples of 8 end in _____, _____, _____, _____ or _____.

TEACHER INFORMATION

NUMBER AND PLACE VALUE

Objective

- Count from 0 in multiples of 50 and 100.

Oral work and mental calculation

- Count on as a class in 10s/50s/100s starting from a two-digit number. Extend to from a three-digit number.

- Count backwards in 10s/50s/100s, starting from a two-digit number. Extend to from a three-digit number.

- Use a class number board. Pick a pupil to choose a number to start from. Count from that number, forwards in tens and then backwards in tens.

Main teaching activity

Counting in 50s and 100s (page 7)

Additional activities suitable for developing the objective

- Make a number line around the perimeter of the classroom or playground. Pupils stand on the number line and follow instructions; for example, 'walk forward 10'.

- Use a number line to respond to questions; for example,
  Count on 30 in tens from 27.
  Count back 20 in tens from 54.
  Count on in tens from 24 to 44. How many tens did you count?

- Complete number sequences; for example, 100, 90, 80, ___, ___ and 0, 50, 100, ___, ___. Explain the sequences.

Answers

1. 0, 10, 20, 30, 40, 50, 60, 70, 80, 90, 100

2. 50, 100, 150, 200, 250, 300, 350, 400, 450, 500, 550, 600, 650, 700, 750, 800, 850, 900, 950, 1000

3. 1000, 900, 800, 700, 600, 500, 400, 300, 200, 100

4. (a) 70, 90, 120, 130, 140
   (b) 120, 100, 70, 50, 20
   (c) 50, 100, 250, 350, 450
   (d) 850, 800, 700, 650, 550, 500
   (e) 1700, 1800, 2000, 2300
   (f) 1400, 1200, 1000, 800

Challenge: 2000, 1800, 1600, 1400, 1200, 1000, 800, 600, 400, 200, 0

COUNTING IN 50s and 100s

1. Count in 10s from 0 to 100.

   _____

   _____

2. Count in 50s from 50 to 1000.

   _____

   _____

   _____

   _____

3. Count in 100s from 1000 to 0.

   _____

   _____

4. Fill in the missing numbers.

   (a) 50, 60, _____, 80, _____, 100, 110, _____, _____, _____, 150

   (b) _____, 110, _____, 90, 80, _____, 60, _____, 40, 30, _____, 10

   (c) 0, _____, _____, 150, 200, _____, 300, _____, 400, _____

   (d) 900, _____, _____, 750, _____, _____, 600, _____, _____, 450, 400

   (e) 1500, 1600, _____, _____, 1900, _____, 2100, 2200, _____

   (f) 1500, _____, 1300, _____, 1100, _____, 900, _____, 700

CHALLENGE

On the back of this sheet, count backwards in 200s from 2000 to 0.

Objective *Counts on and back in 10s, 50s and 100s.*

TEACHER INFORMATION

NUMBER AND PLACE VALUE

Objectives

- Count in multiples of 4, 8, 50 and 100.

- Solve number problems and practical problems involving these ideas.

Oral work and mental calculation

- Count on as a class in 2s/3s/4s/5s/8s/10s/50s/100s starting from a two-digit number. Extend to from a three-digit number.

- Count backwards in 2s/3s/4s/5s/8s/10s/50s/100s, starting from a two-digit number. Extend to from a three-digit number.

- Use a class number board. Pick a pupil to choose a number to start from. Count from that number, forwards in 2s/3s/4s/5s/8s/10s and then backwards in 2s/3s/4s/5s/8s/10s.

Interactive whiteboard activity

Interactive whiteboard activity available to support this copymaster. Visit *www.prim-ed.com*.

Main teaching activity

Number sequences and rules (page 9)

Additional activities suitable for developing the objectives

- Make a number line around the perimeter of the classroom or playground. Pupils stand on the number line and follow instructions; for example, 'walk forward 4'.

- Use a number line to respond to questions; for example,
  Count on 30 in threes from 27.
  Count back 20 in fours from 44.
  Count on in fives from 25 to 55. How many fives did you count?

- Complete number sequences; for example, 327, 330, 333, ____. Explain the sequences.

Answers

1. (a) 80, 84, 88, 92, 96, 100
   (b) 800, 700, 600, 500, 400, 300, 200, 100, 0
   (c) 40, 48, 56, 64, 72, 80, 88, 96, 104, 112, 120
   (d) 40, 44, 48, 52, 56, 60, 64, 68, 72, 76, 80
   (e) 500, 450, 400, 350, 300, 250, 200, 150, 100, 50, 0
   (f) 80, 72, 64, 56, 48, 40, 32, 24, 16, 8, 0

2. (a) Counting backwards in 100s.
   (b) Counting forwards in fours.
   (c) Counting backwards in eights.
   (d) Counting backwards in 50s.
   (e) Counting forwards in 50s.
   (f) Counting forwards in eights.

Challenge: Teacher check

NUMBER SEQUENCES AND RULES

1. Read the rule and complete the pattern.

	Rule	Pattern
(a)	Counting in 4s from 80 to 100.	80, 84, 88,
(b)	Counting backwards in 100s from 800 to 0.	
(c)	Counting in 8s from 40 to 120.	
(d)	Counting in 4s from 40 to 80.	
(e)	Counting backwards in 50s from 500 to 0.	
(f)	Counting backwards in 8s from 80 to 0.	

2. Look at the pattern and write the rule.

	Rule	Pattern
(a)		1000, 900, 800, 700, 600, 500, 400, 300, 200, 100, 0
(b)		20, 24, 28, 32, 36, 40, 44, 48, 52, 56, 60
(c)		80, 72, 64, 56, 48, 40, 32, 24, 16, 8, 0
(d)		1000, 950, 900, 850, 800, 750, 700, 650, 600
(e)		50, 100, 150, 200, 250, 300, 350, 400, 450, 500
(f)		64, 72, 80, 88, 96, 104, 112, 120, 128

CHALLENGE Write your own rule for a number pattern and give it to a friend to see if he/she can work it out.

Objectives • *Identifies the rule used to create a number pattern.* • *Completes a number pattern by following a rule.*

TEACHER INFORMATION

NUMBER AND PLACE VALUE

Objectives

- Find 10 or 100 more or less than a given number.

- Solve number problems and practical problems involving these ideas.

Oral work and mental calculation

- Respond to questions; for example:
  Which is more – 261 or 216?
  Which is longer – 157 m or 517 m?
  Which is lighter – 3.5 kg or 5.5 kg?
  Which is less - £4.63 or £3.46?

- Respond to questions; for example:
  What is 1 more than 485? 569? 873?
  What is 1 less?
  What is 10 more than 437? 678?
  What is 10 less?
  What is 100 more than 678? 428?
  What is 100 less?

- Look at word problems like those in Question 3 and discuss how the answers can be found.

Interactive whiteboard activity

Interactive whiteboard activity available to support this copymaster. Visit *www.prim-ed.com.*

Main teaching activity

More or less (page 11)

Additional activities suitable for developing the objectives

- Give a timed mental calculation test. Repeat the test three times to see if each pupil can beat their own score and time.

- Answer word problems like those in Question 3.

- Pupils write their own word problems. Make them into a class book of problems and challenge another class to solve them.

Answers

1. (a) 23, 569, 841   (b) 21, 567, 839
    (c) 75, 400, 713   (d) 55, 380, 693
    (e) 284, 517, 1023   (f) 84, 317, 823

2. (a) 523   (b) 251   (c) 138   (d) 800
    (e) 152   (f) 1089

3. (a) 68p   (b) 160
    (c) 820   (d) 1055 metres

Challenge: (a) 1100   (b) 1098   (c) 1109
              (d) 1089   (e) 1199   (f) 999

MORE OR LESS

1. Write the number that is ...

(a) 1 more than • 22 ⬚ • 568 ⬚ • 840 ⬚

(b) 1 less than • 22 ⬚ • 568 ⬚ • 840 ⬚

(c) 10 more than • 65 ⬚ • 390 ⬚ • 703 ⬚

(d) 10 less than • 65 ⬚ • 390 ⬚ • 703 ⬚

(e) 100 more than • 184 ⬚ • 417 ⬚ • 923 ⬚

(f) 100 less than • 184 ⬚ • 417 ⬚ • 923 ⬚

2. Write the correct number in the box.

(a) ⬚ $\xrightarrow{\text{1 more is}}$ 524

(b) ⬚ $\xrightarrow{\text{1 less is}}$ 250

(c) ⬚ $\xrightarrow{\text{10 more is}}$ 148

(d) ⬚ $\xrightarrow{\text{10 less is}}$ 790

(e) ⬚ $\xrightarrow{\text{100 more is}}$ 252

(f) ⬚ $\xrightarrow{\text{100 less is}}$ 989

3. Answer the word problems.

(a) Kate has saved 58p. Sam has saved 10p more.
How much money has Sam saved?... ⬚

(b) Hassan has 170 football stickers. Jude has 10 less.
How many stickers does Jude have? .... ⬚

(c) A cinema holds a maximum of 920 people. There are 100 empty seats.
How many people are at the cinema? .... ⬚

(d) Carly walks 955 metres to the shop. Ethan walks 100 metres more.
How far does Ethan walk?.. ⬚

CHALLENGE Write the number that is ...

(a) 1 more ⬚ (b) 1 less ⬚ (c) 10 more ⬚ (d) 10 less ⬚ (e) 100 more ⬚ (f) 100 less ⬚

than the number **1099**.

Objective *Knows the number that is 1, 10 or 100 more or less than a given two- or three-digit number.*

TEACHER INFORMATION

NUMBER AND PLACE VALUE

Objective

- Recognise the place value of each digit in a three-digit number (hundreds, tens and ones).

Oral work and mental calculation

- Hold up a card with a three-digit number on it. Ask the class questions such as, 'What number is on this card?', 'Point to the ten' and 'What number is the unit?'

- Hang a series of three-digit numbers on the class washing line. Give the pupils instructions, such as, 'Go and fetch me the number 56'.

- Say what the digits in three-digit numbers represent; for example, the 4 in 465 represents 400 (or 4 hundreds), the 6 in 65 represents 60 (or 6 tens) and the 5 represents 5 (or 5 ones).

- State the number that is equivalent to 5 hundreds, 7 tens and 4 ones (574).

Main teaching activity

Hundreds, tens and ones (page 13)

Additional activities suitable for developing the objective

- Know Hundreds, Tens and Units/Ones and what each figure in a three-digit number represents.

- Play a matching game of numbers in digits and words. Shuffle the cards well to begin the game.

- Expand numbers; for example, 248 is 200 + 40 + 8. Show the number on an abacus.

- Complete HTU sums using unknown numbers; for example,

  125 = 100 + _____ + 5 or 736 = 700 + 30 + _____

- Use money to explain Tens and Units/Ones; for example, give me 68p in tens and ones or change twenty-two pennies for two tens and two pennies.

Answers

1. (a) 23   (b) 58   (c) 180
   (d) 427   (e) 716

2. (a) 5 tens and 2 ones
   (b) 8 tens and 0 ones
   (c) 1 hundred, 6 tens and 0 ones
   (d) 4 hundreds, 5 tens and 8 ones
   (e) 7 hundreds, 1 ten and 5 ones
   (f) 9 hundreds, 0 tens and 2 ones

3. Teacher check

Challenge: (a) 6   (b) 12   (c) 19   (d) 24

1. Write the number.

   (a) Two tens and three ones = _____

   (b) Five tens and eight ones = _____

   (c) One hundred, eight tens and zero ones = _____

   (d) Four hundreds, two tens and seven ones = _____

   (e) Seven hundreds, one ten and six ones = _____

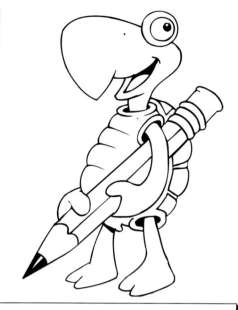

2. Write these numbers as hundreds, tens and ones.

   (a) 52 = _____ tens and _____ ones

   (b) 80 = _____ tens and _____ ones

   (c) 160 = _____ hundred, _____ tens and _____ ones

   (d) 458 = _____ hundreds, _____ tens and _____ ones

   (e) 715 = _____ hundreds, _____ ten and _____ ones

   (f) 902 = _____ hundreds, _____ tens and _____ ones

3. Draw these numbers using place value blocks.

(a)	(b)
381	**295**

CHALLENGE Decide how many tens you would need to show each of these numbers.

(a) 60 _____   (b) 120 _____   (c) 190 _____   (d) 240 _____

Objective   *Knows what each digit in 2- and 3-digit numbers represents.*

TEACHER INFORMATION

NUMBER AND PLACE VALUE

Objective

- Recognise the place value of each digit in a three-digit number (hundreds, tens and ones).

Oral work and mental calculation

- Using an abacus in front of the class, ask each pupil to hold up the number in number cards that is represented on the HTU abacus; for example, 537.

- Respond to questions; for example,
  What does the digit 3 in 364 represent? (300)
  Which number is equivalent to four hundreds, five tens and six ones? (456)
  Make the biggest/smallest number you can with the digits 2, 5 and 3. (532 and 235)

- Use number rods to help pupils see that ten units/ ones make one ten and ten tens make one hundred.

Interactive whiteboard activity

Interactive whiteboard activity available to support this copymaster. Visit *www.prim-ed.com*.

Main teaching activity

Place value – 1 (page 15)

Additional activities suitable for developing the objective

- Partition three-digit numbers; for example,
  527 = 500 + 20 + 7

- Complete the missing number in sums; for example,
  572 = ___ + 70 + 2

- Work with a partner. One pupil holds a number card and the other shows the number either on an abacus or using Base 10 equipment.

Answers

1. (a) 91   (b) 726   (c) 508   (d) 957

2. Teacher check

Challenge: Teacher check

PLACE VALUE – 1

1. Write the numbers represented by these place value blocks. The first one is done for you.

	Hundreds	Tens	Ones	Number
				364
(a)				
(b)				
(c)				
(d)				

2. Represent these numbers by drawing the place value blocks. The first one is done for you.

	Hundreds	Tens	Ones	Number
				258
(a)				514
(b)				706
(c)				149
(d)				390

CHALLENGE On the back of this sheet, represent these numbers by drawing trees for hundreds, sticks for tens and stones for ones.

(a) 315 (b) 174 (c) 609 (d) 28 (e) 260

Objective *Identifies what each digit represents in a three-digit number.*

TEACHER INFORMATION

NUMBER AND PLACE VALUE

Objective

- Recognise the place value of each digit in a three-digit number (hundreds, tens and ones).

Oral work and mental calculation

- Using an abacus in front of the class, ask each pupil to hold up the number in number cards that is represented on the HTU abacus; for example, 537.

- Respond to questions; for example,
  What does the digit 3 in 364 represent? (300)
  Which number is equivalent to four hundreds, five tens and six ones? (456)
  Make the biggest/smallest number you can with the digits 2, 5 and 3. (532 and 235)

- Use number rods to help pupils see that ten units/ ones make one ten and ten tens make one hundred.

Main teaching activity

Place value – 2 (page 17)

Additional activities suitable for developing the objective

- Partition three-digit numbers; for example,
  527 = 500 + 20 + 7

- Complete the missing number in sums; for example,
  572 = ___ + 70 + 2

- Work with a partner. One pupil holds a number card and the other shows the number either on an abacus or using Base 10 equipment.

Answers

1. (a) 5 hundreds   (b) 8 ones
   (c) 9 hundreds   (d) 3 tens
   (e) 5 ones   (f) 0 tens
   (g) 8 tens   (h) 1 one
   (i) 2 hundreds

2. (a) 7 hundreds + 1 ten + 4 ones
   (b) 9 hundreds + 4 tens + 5 ones
   (c) 7 tens + 9 ones
   (d) 2 hundreds + 8 ones
   (e) 6 hundreds + 3 tens
   (f) 8 hundreds + 4 tens + 1 one

3. (a) 74   (b) 392   (c) 951   (d) 190

Challenge: Teacher check

1. State the place value of the number underlined. The first one is done for you.

<u>3</u>12 – *3 hundreds*	(e) 4<u>5</u> –
(a) <u>5</u>72 –	(f) 6<u>0</u>9 –
(b) 14<u>8</u> –	(g) 7<u>8</u>0 –
(c) <u>9</u>24 –	(h) 59<u>1</u> –
(d) <u>3</u>8 –	(i) <u>2</u>53 –

2. Write the numbers in expanded form; e.g. 526 = 5 hundreds + 2 tens + 6 ones.

   (a) 714 _____

   (b) 945 _____

   (c) 79 _____

   (d) 208 _____

   (e) 630 _____

   (f) 841 _____

3. Write the numbers as numerals; e.g. 7 hundreds + 0 tens + 6 ones = 706.

   (a) 7 tens + 4 ones = _____

   (b) 3 hundreds + 9 tens + 2 ones = _____

   (c) 9 hundreds + 5 tens + 1 one = _____

   (d) 1 hundred + 9 tens + 0 ones = _____

CHALLENGE

List six numbers between 200 and 300 on the back of this sheet and write them in expanded form.

Objectives • *Identifies what each digit represents in a three-digit number.* • *Partitions into HTU.*

TEACHER INFORMATION

NUMBER AND PLACE VALUE

Objectives

- Recognise the place value of each digit in a three-digit number (hundreds, tens and ones).

- Solve number problems and practical problems involving these ideas.

Oral work and mental calculation

- Using an abacus in front of the class, ask each pupil to hold up the number in number cards that is represented on the HTU abacus; for example, 537.

- Respond to questions; for example,

  What does the digit 3 in 364 represent? (300)

  Which number is equivalent to four hundreds, five tens and six ones? (456)

  Make the biggest/smallest number you can with the digits 2, 5 and 3. (532 and 235)

- Use number rods to help pupils see that ten units/ones make one ten and ten tens make one hundred.

Interactive whiteboard activity

Interactive whiteboard activity available to support this copymaster. Visit *www.prim-ed.com*.

Main teaching activity

Representing numbers (page 19)

Additional activities suitable for developing the objectives

- Partition three-digit numbers; for example, 527 = 500 + 20 + 7

- Complete the missing number in sums; for example, 572 = _____ + 70 + 2

- Work with a partner. One pupil holds a number card and the other shows the number either on an abacus or using Base 10 equipment.

Answers

1. (a) 80 + 2   (b) 100 + 70 + 5
   (c) 900 + 20 + 6   (d) 300 + 50 + 1
   (e) 400 + 80 + 6   (f) 200 + 90

2. (a) 57   (b) 294   (c) 417   (d) 602
   (e) 835   (f) 942

3. Teacher check

Challenge: Teacher check

REPRESENTING NUMBERS

1. Write these numbers in expanded form; e.g. 749 = 700 + 40 + 9.

   (a) 82 = _____

   (b) 175 = _____

   (c) 926 = _____

   (d) 351 = _____

   (e) 486 = _____

   (f) 290 = _____

2. Write the numbers represented on each abacus.

   (a)
   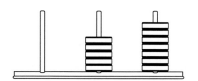
   _____

   (b)

   _____

   (c)
   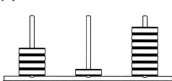
   _____

   (d)
   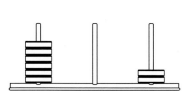
   _____

   (e)
   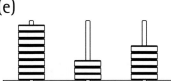
   _____

   (f)
   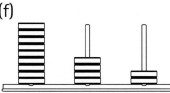
   _____

3. Represent the number on each abacus.

   (a) 159

   (b) 93

   (c) 267

   (d) 403
   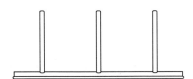

   (e) 815
   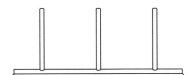

   (f) 729
   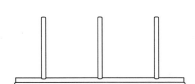

CHALLENGE Show these numbers on an abacus.

(a) Your age

(b) The number of children in your class

(c) Your house number

(d) The number of children in your school

Objectives • *Identifies what each digit represents in a three-digit number.* • *Partitions into HTU.*

TEACHER INFORMATION

NUMBER AND PLACE VALUE

Objective

*   Compare and order numbers up to 1000.

Oral work and mental calculation

*   Count forwards and backwards in ones and also in tens and twos.

*   Respond to questions such as:
    Which number comes after 70? before 39?

*   Use zero when counting.

*   Use a number board or a class 'washing line' to count on and back.

*   Order three-digit number cards from smallest to largest and vice versa.

Main teaching activity

Counting to 1000 (page 21)

Additional activities suitable for developing the objective

*   Give the pupils a two- or three-digit number and ask them to count on in ones and then count back in ones.

*   Make number tracks; for example, fill in the missing numbers:

			46	47	48	49			

*   Respond to questions such as:

    Count on six from 264.
    Count back six from 187.
    How many did you count?

    Count from 153 to 157.
    Count back from 276 to 271.
    How many did you count?

*   Order three-digit number cards from smallest to largest and vice versa.

Answers

1. Teacher check

2. (a) 131, 133, 136, 138
    (b) 414, 418, 420, 424, 428
    (c) 540, 550, 570, 590, 610
    (d) 300, 302, 305, 307
    (e) 708, 707, 705, 703, 700
    (f) 890, 894, 898, 900, 904

3. (a) 363   (b) 285   (c) 327

4. (a) 502   (b) 207   (c) 854

Challenge: (a) 168   (b) 316   (c) 503   (d) 680
             (e) 915   (f) 802

COUNTING TO 1000

1. Fill in the counting chart, counting in 10s to 1000.

10	20		40	50		70		90	100
110		130	140		160	170	180		200
	220		240	250			280	290	
310		330		350	360		380		400
	420	430			460	470		490	
510		530		550		570	580		
610	620		640		660		680		700
	720	730		750	760			790	800
810		830		850		870	880		
910	920		940		960			990	

2. Fill in the missing numbers.

(a) 130, _____, 132, _____, 134, 135, _____, 137, _____, 139.

(b) 410, 412, _____, 416, _____, _____, 422, _____, 426, _____.

(c) 520, 530, _____, _____, 560, _____, 580, _____, 600, _____.

(d) 299, _____, 301, _____, 303, 304, _____, 306, _____, 308.

(e) 710, 709, _____, _____, 706, _____, 704, _____, 702, 701, _____.

(f) 888, _____, 892, _____, 896, _____, _____, 902, _____, 906.

3. Circle the smaller number in each pair.

(a) 641 and 363   (b) 285 and 892   (c) 903 and 327

4. Circle the larger number in each pair.

(a) 502 and 341   (b) 207 and 199   (c) 854 and 293

CHALLENGE Write the number that comes after: (a) 167 _____ (b) 315 _____

(c) 502 _____ (d) 679 _____ (e) 914 _____ (f) 801_____

Objective   *Counts and orders numbers to 1000.*

TEACHER INFORMATION

NUMBER AND PLACE VALUE

Objective

- Compare and order numbers up to 1000.

Oral work and mental calculation

- Place two number cards in front of the class. Ask questions such as:
  What are the numbers?
  Which is more?
  Which is less?

- Make a number line containing three-digit numbers. Remove some of the numbers and ask the pupils which numbers are missing.

- Order three-digit number cards from smallest to largest and vice versa.

- Show the class a number and ask them to hold up the number that comes before it/after it.

Interactive whiteboard activity

Interactive whiteboard activity available to support this copymaster. Visit *www.prim-ed.com*.

Main teaching activity

Comparing and ordering numbers (page 23)

Additional activities suitable for developing the objective

- Working with a partner, one pupil writes ten three-digit numbers on a piece of paper. Their partner has to write the number that comes before and after each given number.

- Order three-digit number cards from smallest to largest and vice versa.

- Work in groups to create a number line from 0–1000.

- Make a washing line containing all numbers between 150 and 170. Remove some of the numbers and hide them around the classroom. Pupils play hide and seek with the numbers. Once the numbers are found they need to be put onto the correct place on the washing line.

- Jumble the numbers on a washing line. Pupils rearrange the numbers into the correct order.

Answers

1. (a) Teacher check; 490, 493, 494, 497, 500, 501, 504, 507, 508
   (b) 504
   (c) 500, 501
   (d) 515

2. (a) 564   (b) 704   (c) 553   (d) 806
   (e) 627   (f) 910

3. (a) 527   (b) 180   (c) 573   (d) 402
   (e) 925   (f) 603

4. (a) 451   (b) 737   (c) 910   (d) 801
   (e) 299, 301, 303, 305
   (f) 548, 550, 551, 553, 554
   (g) 797, 798, 800, 801, 803, 804
   (h) 999, 1000, 1002, 1003, 1005, 1006

Challenge: (a) 120, 312, 321, 488, 567, 590
   (b) 590, 567, 488, 321, 312, 120

COMPARING AND ORDERING NUMBERS

1. Answer the questions about the number line.

   (a) Write the missing numbers in the correct place.

   (b) What number comes between 503 and 505? _____

   (c) What two numbers come between 499 and 502? _____ and _____

   (d) If you counted on 5 more numbers from the end of the number line, what number

   would you be on? _____

2. Circle the larger number in each pair.

   (a) **283** and **564**   (b) **704** and **231**   (c) **525** and **553**

   (d) **608** and **806**   (e) **360** and **627**   (f) **910** and **901**

3. Circle the smaller number in each pair.

   (a) **527** and **845**   (b) **351** and **180**   (c) **573** and **735**

   (d) **402** and **420**   (e) **925** and **952**   (f) **630** and **603**

4. Fill in the missing numbers.

   (a) 450, _____, 452   (b) 736, _____, 738

   (c) 909, _____, 911   (d) 800, _____, 802

   (e) 298, _____, 300, _____, 302, _____, 304, _____, 306

   (f) 547, _____, 549, _____, _____, 552, _____, _____, 555

   (g) 796, _____, _____, 799, _____, _____, 802, _____, _____

   (h) 998, _____, _____, 1001, _____, _____, 1004, _____, _____

CHALLENGE

On the back of the sheet, write the numbers in the cloud ...

(a) from smallest to largest.

(b) from largest to smallest.

567   312
321   488
590   120

Objective   *Compares and orders three-digit numbers.*

TEACHER INFORMATION

NUMBER AND PLACE VALUE

Objectives

- Compare and order numbers up to 1000.

- Solve number problems and practical problems involving these ideas.

Oral work and mental calculation

- Place the number washing line across the classroom. Peg on higher numbers; for example, 800–1000. Shuffle the numbers and ask pupils to reshuffle the numbers into the correct order.

- Give out a selection of number cards; for example, 701–735. Hold up a number (705). Ask pupils with a number higher than this to hold up their number card.

- Write a selection of numbers between 100 and 1000 on the board. Ask pupils to arrange them in order from smallest to largest and vice versa.

- Make a number line containing three-digit numbers. Remove some of the numbers and ask the pupils which numbers are missing.

Main teaching activity

Counting and ordering numbers (page 25)

Additional activities suitable for developing the objectives

- Work in groups to create a number line from 0–1000.

- Shuffle number cards and put them in numerical order.

- On a number line 0–100, marked in tens, mark on other numbers; for example, 28, 73.

- Position one- and two-digit numbers on a blank hundred square.

Answers

1. (a) 451, 453, 456, 458, 459
   (b) 700, 720, 750, 770, 780, 800
   (c) 154, 158, 160, 164, 168
   (d) 201, 204, 206, 207, 209, 210
   (e) 200, 400, 700, 800, 1000
   (f) 60, 100, 140, 180
   (g) 798, 796, 795, 792, 790

2. (a) 5, 10, 20, 30, 40, 55, 75, 95
   (b) 100, 200, 400, 500, 600, 700, 900
   (c) 302, 304, 321, 335, 356, 378, 399
   (d) 120, 312, 437, 488, 567, 690, 981

3. (a) 1000, 800, 750, 600, 500, 450, 350, 250, 100, 50
   (b) 999, 989, 976, 954, 951, 946, 930, 917, 913, 902

Challenge: 609, 613, 626, 627, 628, 642, 659, 673, 678, 685, 694, 699

1. Fill in the missing numbers.

   (a) 450, _____, 452, _____, 454, 455, _____, 457, _____, _____, 460

   (b) _____, 710, _____, 730, 740, _____, 760, _____, _____, 790, _____

   (c) 150, 152, _____, 156, _____, _____, 162, _____, 166, _____, 170

   (d) 200, _____, 202, 203, _____, 205, _____, _____, 208, _____, _____

   (e) 100, _____, 300, _____, 500, 600, _____, _____, 900, _____

   (f) 20, 40, _____, 80, _____, 120, _____, 160, _____, 200

   (g) 800, 799, _____, 797, _____, _____, 794, 793, _____, 791, _____

2. Write these numbers in order from smallest to largest.

   (a) 95, 20, 55, 5, 40, 75, 10, 30   (b)   200, 600, 100, 400, 700, 500, 900

   _____   _____

   _____   _____

   (c) 335, 378, 321, 399, 304, 356, 302   (d)   567, 312, 488, 690, 120, 437, 981

   _____   _____

   _____   _____

3. Write these numbers in order from largest to smallest.

   (a) 50, 350, 600, 1000, 450, 500, 750, 100, 250, 800

   _____

   (b) 913, 976, 999, 954, 902, 951, 989, 946, 917, 930

   _____

CHALLENGE

Write these numbers in order from smallest to largest.
628, 659, 673, 613, 642, 609, 678, 694, 626, 627, 699, 685

TEACHER INFORMATION

NUMBER AND PLACE VALUE

Objective

- Identify, represent and estimate numbers using different representations.

Oral work and mental calculation

- Look at collections of objects; for example, beads, buttons, 2-D shapes. Estimate how many objects are in the collection. Discuss ways of making sensible estimates.

Main teaching activity

Estimating (Groups of 5) (page 27)

Additional activities suitable for developing the objective

- Group collections of objects in twos, fives and tens; for example, beads, buttons, sugar cubes.

- Investigate the 'best' way to group and count: all the pupils in the class/school, the books on the shelf, the pencils in the pot.

Answers

1. (a) 20   (b) 16   (c) 35
   (d) 23   (e) 17   (f) 28

2. 37 raindrops

Challenge: Teacher check

ESTIMATING (GROUPS OF 5)

1. An estimate is a guess. Estimate the size of these groups. Circle groups of five and write the answer. Was your estimate close?

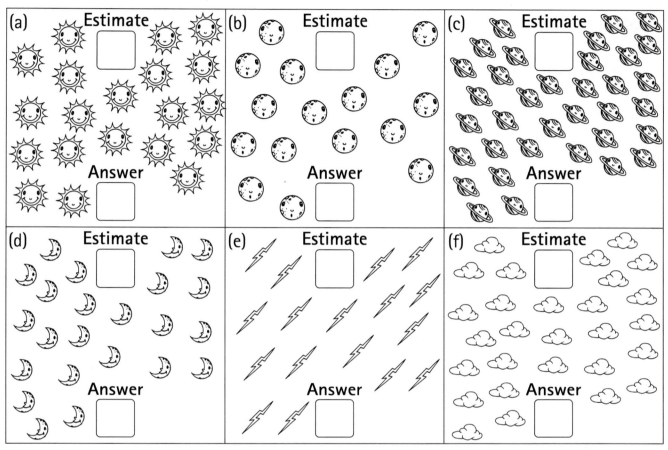

(a) Estimate [ ] Answer [ ]

(b) Estimate [ ] Answer [ ]

(c) Estimate [ ] Answer [ ]

(d) Estimate [ ] Answer [ ]

(e) Estimate [ ] Answer [ ]

(f) Estimate [ ] Answer [ ]

2. Estimate how many raindrops there are. Then circle groups of five to check your estimate.

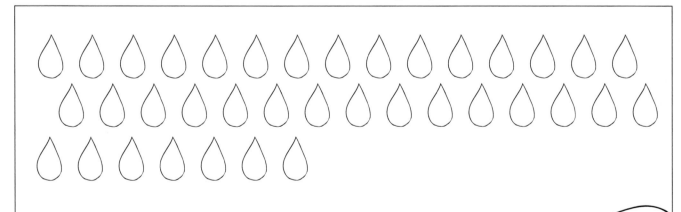

CHALLENGE

Estimate how many pencils you have. _____

Count how many pencils you have. _____

Was your estimate close? [yes | no]

Objective *Estimates and counts reliably by grouping.*

TEACHER INFORMATION

NUMBER AND PLACE VALUE

Objectives

- Identify, represent and estimate numbers using different representations.
- Solve number problems and practical problems involving these ideas.

Oral work and mental calculation

- Look at collections of objects; for example, beads, buttons, 2-D shapes. Estimate how many objects are in the collection. Discuss ways of making sensible estimates.

Main teaching activity

Estimating (Groups of 10 and 100) (page 29)

Additional activities suitable for developing the objectives

- Group collections of objects in twos, fives and tens; for example, beads, buttons, sugar cubes.
- Investigate the 'best' way to group and count: all the pupils in the class/school, the books on the shelf, the pencils in the pot.

Answers

1. (a) 20   (b) 30   (c) 14   (d) 43
2. (a) 100   (b) 210   (c) 120   (d) 300

Challenge: Teacher check

ESTIMATING (GROUPS OF 10 AND 100)

1. Estimate and then group these pictures into lots of 10.

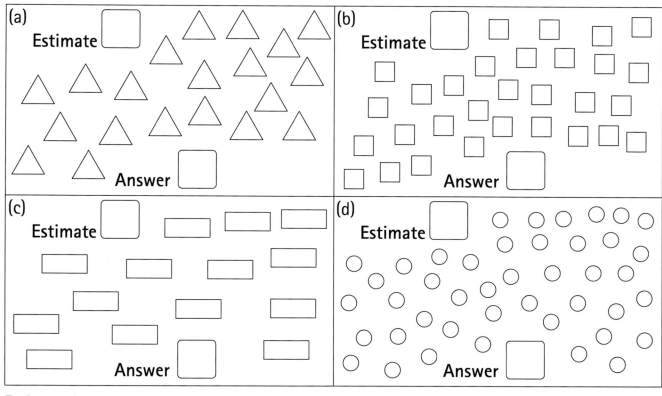

(a) Estimate ☐   Answer ☐

(b) Estimate ☐   Answer ☐

(c) Estimate ☐   Answer ☐

(d) Estimate ☐   Answer ☐

2. Estimate how many hundreds there are by grouping the blocks of 10.

(a) Estimate ☐   Answer ☐

(b) Estimate ☐   Answer ☐

(c) Estimate ☐   Answer ☐

(d) Estimate ☐   Answer ☐

CHALLENGE Estimate how many counters there are in a container.

Count them out into lots of 10. How many lots of 10? _____   Answer = _____

Objectives • *Estimates groups of objects.* • *Calculates the number of objects by grouping into lots of 10.*

TEACHER INFORMATION

NUMBER AND PLACE VALUE

Objective

- Read and write numbers up to 1000 in numerals and words.

Oral work and mental calculation

- Hold up a card with a two- or three-digit number on it. Ask the class, 'What number is on this card?'

- Hang a series of two- or three-digit numbers on the class washing line. Give the pupils instructions, such as, 'Go and fetch me the number 70'.

- Ask a pupil to point out a given number on the class number board or on their own hundred square.

- Pin numbers to half of the pupils and tell them to find their matching words (which would be pinned on the other half of the pupils).

Interactive whiteboard activity

Interactive whiteboard activity available to support this copymaster. Visit *www.prim-ed.com*.

Main teaching activity

Words and numbers (100 to 1000) (page 31)

Additional activities suitable for developing the objective

- Know Hundreds, Tens and Units/Ones and what each figure in a three–digit number represents.

- Play a matching game of numbers in digits and words. Shuffle the cards well to begin the game.

- Expand numbers; for example, 268 is 200 + 60 + 8. Show the number on an abacus.

- Use money to explain Tens and Units/Ones; for example, give me 68p in tens and ones or change twenty-two pennies for two tens and two pennies.

Answers

1. Teacher check

Challenge: Teacher check

WORDS AND NUMBERS (100 TO 1000)

Copy the words, then glue the numbers below next to the correct word.

(a)
one hundred

(b)
two hundred

(c)
three hundred

(d)
four hundred

(e)
five hundred

(f)
six hundred

(g)
seven hundred

(h)
eight hundred

(i)
nine hundred

(j)
one thousand

Careful! The numbers are jumbled.

300	900	700	100	500	1000	600	800	400	200

CHALLENGE

Using the tens and ones blocks, make these numbers – 12, 17, 19, 27 and 29.

Objective   *Reads, writes and identifies numerals between 100 and 1000.*

TEACHER INFORMATION

NUMBER AND PLACE VALUE

Objective

- Read and write numbers up to 1000 in numerals and words.

Oral work and mental calculation

- Hold up a card with a two- or three-digit number on it. Ask the class, 'What number is on this card?'

- Hang a series of two- or three-digit numbers on the class washing line. Give the pupils instructions, such as, 'Go and fetch me the number 70'.

- Ask a pupil to point out a given number on the class number board or on their own hundred square.

- Pin numbers to half of the pupils and tell them to find their matching words (which would be pinned on the other half of the pupils).

Main teaching activity

Reading and writing numbers (page 33)

Additional activities suitable for developing the objective

- Know Hundreds, Tens and Units/Ones and what each figure in a three–digit number represents.

- Play a matching game of numbers in digits and words. Shuffle the cards well to begin the game.

- Expand numbers; for example, 268 is 200 + 60 + 8. Show the number on an abacus.

- Use money to explain Tens and Units/Ones; for example, give me 68p in tens and ones or change twenty-two pennies for two tens and two pennies.

Answers

1. (a) sixty-three
   (b) twenty-seven
   (c) one hundred and thirty-five
   (d) five hundred and twenty
   (e) nine hundred and forty-three

2. (a) 36   (b) 98   (c) 215
   (d) 432   (e) 170   (f) 781

3. (a) twelve
   (b) twenty-six
   (c) one hundred and forty-five
   (d) two hundred and sixty
   (e) five hundred and eighty-nine
   (f) nine hundred and twenty-seven

Challenge: two thousand, three hundred and fifty-eight

READING AND WRITING NUMBERS

1. Draw lines to match the numerals to the number words.

(a) | 63 | one hundred and thirty-five

(b) | 27 | nine hundred and forty-three

(c) | 135 | sixty-three

(d) | 520 | twenty-seven

(e) | 943 | five hundred and twenty

2. Write the number next to the words.

(a) thirty-six ☐   (b) ninety-eight ☐

(c) two hundred and fifteen ☐   (d) four hundred and thirty-two ☐

(e) one hundred and seventy ☐   (f) seven hundred and eighty-one ☐

3. Write the words for these numbers.

(a) 12 _____

(b) 26 _____

(c) 145 _____

(d) 260 _____

(e) 589 _____

(f) 927 _____

CHALLENGE

Write this number in words.

2358 _____

Objective *Reads and writes numbers as numerals and words.*

TEACHER INFORMATION

NUMBER AND PLACE VALUE

Objectives

- Read and write numbers up to 1000 in numerals and words.

- Solve number problems and practical problems involving these ideas.

Oral work and mental calculation

- Use a number washing line across the classroom to peg numerals with matching number words.

- Pin numbers to half of the class. Pin the matching number words to the other half of the class. Pupils have to find their matching partner.

- The teacher has a set of flashcards showing matching numbers and words to 1000. The teacher gives the numbers out to the class. The teacher holds up each number word in turn. The pupil with the matching number card holds it up.

Main teaching activity

Numbers and words (page 35)

Additional activities suitable for developing the objectives

- Working in pairs, one pupil writes down five numbers between 1–1000 on a piece of paper. The partner has to write the corresponding number word next to each number.

- Make sets of number cards with matching number words. Place all the cards face down. Pupils take it in turns to turn over two cards. If they match a number to its number word then they keep the cards. If they do not match then the cards are turned face down again. The game continues until all cards have been matched. The winner is the pupil with the most cards.

- Play numbers bingo with cards that have numbers and number words written on them. As the teacher calls out each number, the pupil has to cover the appropriate number or word on their card with a counter.

Answers

1. (a) 37   (b) 104   (c) 329   (d) 614
    (e) 985   (f) 246   (g) 491   (h) 762

2. (a) sixty-three
    (b) one hundred and nine
    (c) four hundred and ninety-five
    (d) six hundred and seventeen
    (e) two hundred and thirty
    (f) seven hundred and eighty-one
    (g) eight hundred and nine
    (h) four hundred and twelve

3. (a) 356   (b) 2411   (c) 901   (d) 8153

Challenge: Teacher check

NUMBERS AND WORDS

1. Write the numbers for these words.

   (a) thirty-seven _____

   (b) one hundred and four _____

   (c) three hundred and twenty-nine _____

   (d) six hundred and fourteen _____

   (e) nine hundred and eighty-five _____

   (f) two hundred and forty-six _____

   (g) four hundred and ninety-one _____

   (h) seven hundred and sixty-two _____

2. Write the words for these numbers.

   (a) 63 _____

   (b) 109 _____

   (c) 495 _____

   (d) 617 _____

   _____

   _____

   (e) 230 _____

   (f) 781 _____

   _____

   _____

   (g) 809 _____

   (h) 412 _____

   _____

   _____

3. Draw lines to match the words with the numbers.

   (a) three hundred and fifty-six •   • 8153

   (b) two thousand, four hundred and eleven •   • 356

   (c) nine hundred and one •   • 2411

   (d) eight thousand, one hundred and fifty-three •   • 901

CHALLENGE

On the back of this sheet, see how many little words you can make by rearranging the letters in the word 'THOUSAND'.

Objective   *Reads and writes whole numbers to one thousand.*

TEACHER INFORMATION

ADDITION AND SUBTRACTION

Objective

- Add numbers mentally, including:
  - a three-digit number and ones
  - a three-digit number and tens
  - a three-digit number and hundreds.

Oral work and mental calculation

- Count out loud in ones, tens and hundreds, from zero and random starting points.

- Respond to questions; for example,

  What is one more than 485? 569? 873?

  What is ten more than 437? 678? 924?

  What is one hundred more than 676? 320? 548?

  Which tens number comes after 320? 480?

  Which hundreds number comes after 320? 480?

- Hold up a three-digit number card and a multiple of 10 or 100. Mentally add the two numbers.

Main teaching activity

Adding numbers mentally (page 37)

Additional activities suitable for developing the objective

- Complete number sequences; for example, 410, 420, ___, ___, 450, ___, 470. Explain the sequences.

- Complete word problems involving adding tens or hundreds; for example,

  Sam walks 545 metres to school. Kasim walks 300 metres more. How far does Kasim walk?

  Kate has 523 football stickers. Sara has 70 more. How many stickers does Sara have?

Answers

1. (a) 432	(b) 308	(c) 295	(d) 164
(e) 956	(f) 783	(g) 550	(h) 861

2. (a) 441	(b) 317	(c) 304	(d) 173
(e) 665	(f) 792	(g) 559	(h) 870

3. (a) 531	(b) 407	(c) 394	(d) 263
(e) 1055	(f) 882	(g) 649	(h) 960

4. (a) 296	(b) 748	(c) 407	(d) 190
(e) 522	(f) 869	(g) 733	(h) 920
(i) 352	(j) 596	(k) 392	(l) 775
(m) 154	(n) 697	(o) 283	(p) 894
(q) 501	(r) 976	(s) 895	(t) 734
(u) 925	(v) 707	(w) 990	(x) 821
(y) 784	(z) 681		

Challenge: (a) 26 (b) 160 (c) 1100

ADDING NUMBERS MENTALLY

1. Add **one** to each of these numbers.

   (a) 431 = _____   (b) 307 = _____   (c) 294 = _____   (d) 163 = _____

   (e) 955 = _____   (f) 782 = _____   (g) 549 = _____   (h) 860 = _____

2. Add **ten** to each of these numbers.

   (a) 431 = _____   (b) 307 = _____   (c) 294 = _____   (d) 163 = _____

   (e) 655 = _____   (f) 782 = _____   (g) 549 = _____   (h) 860 = _____

3. Add **one hundred** to each of these numbers.

   (a) 431 = _____   (b) 307 = _____   (c) 294 = _____   (d) 163 = _____

   (e) 955 = _____   (f) 782 = _____   (g) 549 = _____   (h) 860 = _____

4. Complete these mental addition sums.

   (a) 293 + 3 = _____   (b) 745 + 3 = _____   (c) 402 + 5 = _____

   (d) 186 + 4 = _____   (e) 517 + 5 = _____   (f) 860 + 9 = _____

   (g) 725 + 8 = _____   (h) 914 + 6 = _____   (i) 345 + 7 = _____

   (j) 546 + 50 = _____   (k) 382 + 10 = _____   (l) 745 + 30 = _____

   (m) 124 + 30 = _____   (n) 617 + 80 = _____   (o) 263 + 20 = _____

   (p) 804 + 90 = _____   (q) 481 + 20 = _____   (r) 936 + 40 = _____

   (s) 595 + 300 = _____   (t) 334 + 400 = _____   (u) 125 + 800 = _____

   (v) 207 + 500 = _____   (w) 890 + 100 = _____   (x) 321 + 500 = _____

   (y) 384 + 400 = _____   (z) 481 + 200 = _____

CHALLENGE

Use mental calculation to add the numbers in each cloud.

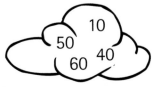

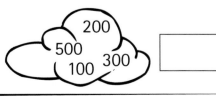

Objective   *Adds ones, tens and hundreds to three-digit numbers.*

TEACHER INFORMATION

ADDITION AND SUBTRACTION

Objective

- Subtract numbers mentally, including:
  - a three-digit number and ones
  - a three-digit number and tens
  - a three-digit number and hundreds.

Oral work and mental calculation

- Count backwards in ones, tens and hundreds, from varying starting points.

- Respond to questions; for example,

  What is one less than 485? 569? 873?

  What is ten less than 437? 678? 924?

  What is one hundred less than 676? 320? 548?

  Which tens number comes before 320? 480?

  Which hundreds number comes before 320? 480?

- Hold up a three-digit number card and a multiple of 10 or 100. Mentally subtract the two numbers.

Main teaching activity

Subtracting numbers mentally (page 39)

Additional activities suitable for developing the objective

- Complete number sequences; for example, 470, 460, ___, ___, 430, ___, 410. Explain the sequences.

- Complete word problems involving subtracting tens or hundreds; for example,

  Sam walks 890 metres to school. Kasim walks 300 metres less. How far does Kasim walk?

  Kate has 683 football stickers. Sara has 70 less. How many stickers does Sara have?

Answers

1.	(a) 430	(b) 306	(c) 293	(d) 162
	(e) 954	(f) 781	(g) 548	(h) 859
2.	(a) 421	(b) 297	(c) 284	(d) 153
	(e) 945	(f) 772	(g) 539	(h) 850
3.	(a) 331	(b) 207	(c) 194	(d) 63
	(e) 855	(f) 682	(g) 449	(h) 760
4.	(a) 290	(b) 741	(c) 404	(d) 182
	(e) 512	(f) 851	(g) 717	(h) 908
	(i) 338	(j) 526	(k) 372	(l) 715
	(m) 124	(n) 617	(o) 243	(p) 714
	(q) 381	(r) 896	(s) 295	(t) 234
	(u) 125	(v) 207	(w) 790	(x) 221
	(y) 84	(z) 281		

Challenge: Maria = 786, David = 726, Paula = 676

SUBTRACTING NUMBERS MENTALLY

1. Subtract **one** from each of these numbers.

   (a) 431 = _____   (b) 307 = _____   (c) 294 = _____   (d) 163 = _____

   (e) 955 = _____   (f) 782 = _____   (g) 549 = _____   (h) 860 = _____

2. Subtract **ten** from each of these numbers.

   (a) 431 = _____   (b) 307 = _____   (c) 294 = _____   (d) 163 = _____

   (e) 955 = _____   (f) 782 = _____   (g) 549 = _____   (h) 860 = _____

3. Subtract **one hundred** from each of these numbers.

   (a) 431 = _____   (b) 307 = _____   (c) 294 = _____   (d) 163 = _____

   (e) 955 = _____   (f) 782 = _____   (g) 549 = _____   (h) 860 = _____

4. Complete these mental subtraction sums.

   (a) 293 – 3 = _____   (b) 745 – 4 = _____   (c) 409 – 5 = _____

   (d) 186 – 4 = _____   (e) 517 – 5 = _____   (f) 860 – 9 = _____

   (g) 725 – 8 = _____   (h) 914 – 6 = _____   (i) 345 – 7 = _____

   (j) 576 – 50 = _____   (k) 382 – 10 = _____   (l) 745 – 30 = _____

   (m) 154 – 30 = _____   (n) 697 – 80 = _____   (o) 263 – 20 = _____

   (p) 804 – 90 = _____   (q) 431 – 50 = _____   (r) 936 – 40 = _____

   (s) 595 – 300 = _____   (t) 634 – 400 = _____   (u) 925 – 800 = _____

   (v) 707 – 500 = _____   (w) 890 – 100 = _____   (x) 721 – 500 = _____

   (y) 684 – 600 = _____   (z) 481 – 200 = _____

CHALLENGE   Fred has 986 football stickers.

Maria has 200 less. Maria has _____ stickers.

David has 60 less than Maria. David has _____ stickers.

Paula has 50 less than David. Paula has _____ stickers.

Objective   *Subtracts ones, tens and hundreds from three-digit numbers.*

TEACHER INFORMATION

ADDITION AND SUBTRACTION

Objective

- Add numbers with up to three digits, using formal written methods of columnar addition.

Oral work and mental calculation

- Practise rapid recall of addition facts for each number to 10.

- Discuss methods for completing TU + TU sums, without and with trading. Extend to HTU + HTU sums.

- Demonstrate the expanded method in columns for completing TU + TU sums. Extend this to HTU + HTU sums.

Interactive whiteboard activity

Interactive whiteboard activity available to support this copymaster. Visit *www.prim-ed.com*.

Main teaching activity

Expanded column addition (page 41)

Additional activities suitable for developing the objective

- Transfer addition sums to a vertical layout; for example, change 235 + 412 = 647 to

$$
\begin{array}{r}
235 \\
+\ 412 \\
\hline
647 \\
\hline
\end{array}
$$

- Practise TU + TU sums, using pencil and paper methods, without and with trading. Extend to HTU + HTU sums.

Answers

1. (a) 61   (b) 65   (c) 94   (d) 96
   (e) 82   (f) 138

2. (a) 597   (b) 691   (c) 818   (d) 894
   (e) 921   (f) 742

Challenge: (a) 98 (b) 161 (c) 791

EXPANDED COLUMN ADDITION

1. Use expanded column addition to solve these sums.

Example:

```
    37
+   15
    ___
    12    (Add the ones: 7 + 5)
    40    (Add the tens: 30 + 10)
    ___
    52    (Add the two answers: 12 + 40)
```

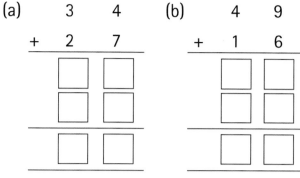

(a) 3 4
   + 2 7

(b)   4 9
      + 1 6

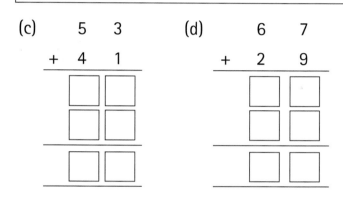

(c)   5 3
     + 4 1

(d)   6 7
     + 2 9

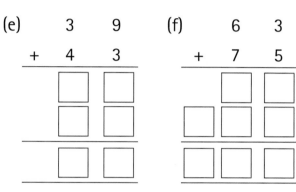

(e)   3 9
     + 4 3

(f)   6 3
     + 7 5

2. Use expanded column addition to solve these sums.

Example:

```
    235
+   412
    ___
      7    (Add the ones: 5 + 2)
     40    (Add the tens: 30 + 10)
    600    (Add the hundreds: 200 + 400)
    ___
    647    (Add the three answers: 7 + 40 + 600)
```

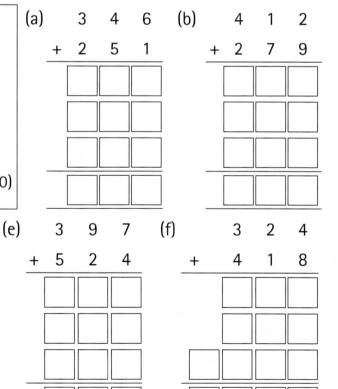

(a) 3 4 6
   + 2 5 1

(b) 4 1 2
   + 2 7 9

(c) 5 2 0
   + 2 9 8

(d) 5 8 9
   + 3 0 5

(e) 3 9 7
   + 5 2 4

(f) 3 2 4
   + 4 1 8

 Solve these addition sums on the back of the sheet.

(a) 73 + 25   (b) 93 + 68   (c) 284 + 507

Objective *Solves addition sums using expanded column addition.*

TEACHER INFORMATION

ADDITION AND SUBTRACTION

Objective

- Add numbers with up to three digits, using formal written methods of columnar addition.

Oral work and mental calculation

- Practise rapid recall of addition facts for each number to 10.

- Use Base 10 material to illustrate addition with trading.

- Discuss methods for completing TU + TU sums, without and with trading. Extend to HTU + HTU sums.

- Demonstrate the column method for completing TU + TU sums. Extend this to HTU + HTU sums.

Main teaching activity

Column addition with trading – 1 (page 43)

Additional activities suitable for developing the objective

- Transfer addition sums to a vertical layout; for example, change 235 + 412 = 647 to

$$
\begin{array}{r}
235 \\
+\ 412 \\
\hline
647 \\
\hline
\end{array}
$$

- Practise TU + TU sums, using pencil and paper methods, without and with trading. Extend to HTU + HTU sums.

Answers

1. (a) 41   (b) 35   (c) 43   (d) 60
   (e) 965   (f) 1091   (g) 764   (h) 993
   (i) 763   (j) 891

   Challenge: (a) 860   (b) 773   (c) 1385   (d) 1390

When two numbers add up to more than 10, we need to trade the 10 ones for 1 ten and write it in the tens column. Look at the example.

8 + 6 = 14, so the 10 from the number 14 is traded into the tens column and added with the tens.

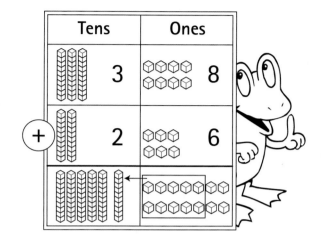

Tens	Ones
3	8
+ 2	6

1. Add these numbers and remember to trade.

(a)

Tens	Ones
2	7
+ 1	4

(b)

Tens	Ones
1	9
+ 1	6

(c)

Tens	Ones
2	5
+ 1	8

(d)

Tens	Ones
3	6
+ 2	4

(e)

Hundreds	Tens	Ones
5	3	9
+ 4	2	6

(f)

Hundreds	Tens	Ones
8	5	3
+ 2	3	8

(g)

Hundreds	Tens	Ones
6	4	8
+ 1	1	6

(h)

Hundreds	Tens	Ones
2	5	7
+ 7	3	6

(i)

Hundreds	Tens	Ones
4	3	4
+ 3	2	9

(j)

Hundreds	Tens	Ones
5	4	9
+ 3	4	2

CHALLENGE

On the back of this sheet, set these addition sums out vertically and solve them.

(a) 632 + 228   (b) 456 + 317   (c) 946 + 439   (d) 867 + 523

TEACHER INFORMATION

ADDITION AND SUBTRACTION

Objective

- Add numbers with up to three digits, using formal written methods of columnar addition.

Oral work and mental calculation

- Practise rapid recall of addition facts for each number to 10.

- Use Base 10 material to illustrate addition with trading.

- Discuss methods for completing TU + TU sums, without and with trading. Extend to HTU + HTU sums.

- Demonstrate the column method for completing TU + TU sums. Extend this to HTU + HTU sums.

Main teaching activity

Column addition with trading – 2 (page 45)

Additional activities suitable for developing the objective

- Transfer addition sums to a vertical layout; for example, change 235 + 412 = 647 to

$$
\begin{array}{r}
235 \\
+\ 412 \\
\hline
647 \\
\hline
\end{array}
$$

- Practise TU + TU sums, using pencil and paper methods, without and with trading. Extend to HTU + HTU sums.

Answers

1. (a) 250   (b) 271   (c) 380   (d) 373
   (e) 584   (f) 584   (g) 628   (h) 718
   (i) 865   (j) 749   (k) 924   (l) 934

2. (a) 384   (b) 327   (c) 540   (d) 465
   (e) 833   (f) 842   (g) 918

Challenge: (a) 375   (b) 813   (c) 759   (d) 642

COLUMN ADDITION WITH TRADING – 2

1. Add these 3-digit numbers. Remember to start in the ones column. For some of them, you may need to trade 10 ones for 1 ten, or 10 tens for 1 hundred.

(a)

Hundreds	Tens	Ones
1	0	8
1	4	2

(b)

Hundreds	Tens	Ones
1	4	9
1	2	2

(c)

Hundreds	Tens	Ones
2	5	2
1	2	8

(d)

Hundreds	Tens	Ones
2	0	6
1	6	7

(e)

Hundreds	Tens	Ones
3	1	9
2	6	5

(f)

Hundreds	Tens	Ones
2	5	8
3	2	6

(g)

Hundreds	Tens	Ones
4	4	1
1	8	7

(h)

Hundreds	Tens	Ones
4	6	7
2	5	1

(i)

Hundreds	Tens	Ones
5	5	7
3	0	8

(j)

Hundreds	Tens	Ones
4	8	5
2	6	4

(k)

Hundreds	Tens	Ones
6	4	9
2	7	5

(l)

Hundreds	Tens	Ones
5	7	8
3	5	6

2. Add these 3-digit numbers.

e.g.   348
+ 270
——
618

(a)   249
+ 135

(b)   152
+ 175

(c)   360
+ 180

(d)   239
+ 226

(e)   485
+ 348

(f)   674
+ 168

(g)   539
+ 379

CHALLENGE On the back of this sheet, set these sums out vertically and solve them. Remember, you may need to trade.

(a) 257 + 118   (b) 596 + 217   (c) 494 + 265   (d) 397 + 245

Objective *Uses written methods to solve addition problems involving trading.*

Primary Maths   Prim-Ed Publishing   www.prim-ed.com   45

TEACHER INFORMATION

ADDITION AND SUBTRACTION

Objective

- Subtract numbers with up to three digits, using formal written methods of columnar subtraction.

Oral work and mental calculation

- Practise counting up from the smaller number to the larger number; for example, 605 – 596 – count up from 596 to 605 to give the answer 9.

- Discuss methods for completing TU – TU sums, without and with trading. Extend to HTU – HTU sums.

- Demonstrate the expanded method in columns for completing TU – TU sums. Extend this to HTU – HTU sums.

Interactive whiteboard activity

Interactive whiteboard activity available to support this copymaster. Visit *www.prim-ed.com*.

Main teaching activity

Subtraction – partitioning – 1 (page 47)

Additional activities suitable for developing the objective

- Transfer subtraction sums to a vertical layout; for example, change 786 – 374 = 412 to

```
  786
-  374
 _____
  412
```

- Practise TU - TU sums, using pencil and paper methods, without and with trading. Extend to HTU - HTU sums.

Answers

1. (a) 34   (b) 16   (c) 34   (d) 11   (e) 63

2. (a) 25   (b) 5   (c) 25   (d) 6   (e) 27   (f) 58

Challenge: (a) 328   (b) 381   (c) 381

SUBTRACTION – PARTITIONING – 1

1. Use the expanded method to solve these subtraction sums.

Example: 49 – 25

$$40 + 9$$
$$- \ 20 + 5$$
$$\overline{20 + 4 = 24}$$

(a) 48 – 14

☐ + ☐
– ☐ + ☐
☐ + ☐ = ☐

(b) 59 – 43

☐ + ☐
– ☐ + ☐
☐ + ☐ = ☐

(c) 65 – 31

☐ + ☐
– ☐ + ☐
☐ + ☐ = ☐

(d) 78 – 67

☐ + ☐
– ☐ + ☐
☐ + ☐ = ☐

(e) 97 – 34

☐ + ☐
– ☐ + ☐
☐ + ☐ = ☐

2. Use the expanded method to solve these subtraction sums with trading.

Example: 45 – 29

$$40 + 5$$
$$- \ 20 + 9$$

! *The top ones number is smaller than the bottom ones number. We need to trade a ten from the tens column and place it in the ones column.*

$$\overset{30}{\cancel{40}} + \overset{15}{\cancel{5}}$$
$$- \ 20 + 9$$
$$\overline{10 + 6 = 16}$$

(a) 42 – 17

☐ + ☐
– ☐ + ☐
☐ + ☐ = ☐

(b) 54 – 49

☐ + ☐
– ☐ + ☐
☐ + ☐ = ☐

(c) 61 – 36

☐ + ☐
– ☐ + ☐
☐ + ☐ = ☐

(d) 72 – 66

☐ + ☐
– ☐ + ☐
☐ + ☐ = ☐

(e) 81 – 54

☐ + ☐
– ☐ + ☐
☐ + ☐ = ☐

(f) 95 – 37

☐ + ☐
– ☐ + ☐
☐ + ☐ = ☐

CHALLENGE Solve these subtraction sums on the back of the sheet.

(a) 569 – 241   (b) 685 – 304   (c) 894 – 513

Objective   *Solves subtraction sums using the expanded method.*

ADDITION AND SUBTRACTION

Objective

- Subtract numbers with up to three digits, using formal written methods of columnar subtraction.

Oral work and mental calculation

- Practise counting up from the smaller number to the larger number; for example, 605 – 596 – count up from 596 to 605 to give the answer 9.

- Discuss methods for completing TU – TU sums, without and with trading. Extend to HTU – HTU sums.

- Demonstrate the expanded method in columns for completing TU – TU sums. Extend this to HTU – HTU sums.

Main teaching activity

Subtraction – partitioning 2 (page 49)

Additional activities suitable for developing the objective

- Transfer subtraction sums to a vertical layout; for example, change 786 – 374 = 412 to

```
   786
 - 374
 -----
   412
```

- Practise TU - TU sums, using pencil and paper methods, without and with trading. Extend to HTU - HTU sums.

Answers

1. (a) 524   (b) 333   (c) 164   (d) 654

2. (a) 425   (b) 237   (c) 362   (d) 265
   (e) 276   (f) 643

Challenge: (a) 336   (b) 645   (c) 577

1. Use the expanded method to solve these subtraction sums.

Example: 578 – 251

500 + 70 + 8
− 200 + 50 + 1
_____
300 + 20 + 7 = 327

(a)   658 – 134

☐ + ☐ + ☐
− ☐ + ☐ + ☐
_____
☐ + ☐ + ☐ = ☐

(b)   657 – 324

☐ + ☐ + ☐
− ☐ + ☐ + ☐
_____
☐ + ☐ + ☐ = ☐

(c)   785 – 621

☐ + ☐ + ☐
− ☐ + ☐ + ☐
_____
☐ + ☐ + ☐ = ☐

(d)   978 – 324

☐ + ☐ + ☐
− ☐ + ☐ + ☐
_____
☐ + ☐ + ☐ = ☐

2. Use the expanded method to solve these subtraction sums with trading.

Example: 542 – 317

500 + 40 + 2
− 300 + 10 + 7

! *The top ones number is smaller than the bottom ones number. We need to trade a ten from the tens column and place it in the ones column.*

          30   12
500 + 4̶0̶ + 2̶
− 300 + 10 + 7
_____
200 + 20 + 5 = 225

(a)   652 – 227

☐ + ☐ + ☐
− ☐ + ☐ + ☐
_____
☐ + ☐ + ☐ = ☐

(b)   543 – 306

☐ + ☐ + ☐
− ☐ + ☐ + ☐
_____
☐ + ☐ + ☐ = ☐

(c)   691 – 329

☐ + ☐ + ☐
− ☐ + ☐ + ☐
_____
☐ + ☐ + ☐ = ☐

! *For the following sums, the top tens number is smaller than the bottom tens number. You need to trade a hundred from the hundreds column and place it in the tens column.*

(d)   728 – 463

☐ + ☐ + ☐
− ☐ + ☐ + ☐
_____
☐ + ☐ + ☐ = ☐

(e)   819 – 543

☐ + ☐ + ☐
− ☐ + ☐ + ☐
_____
☐ + ☐ + ☐ = ☐

(f)   927 – 284

☐ + ☐ + ☐
− ☐ + ☐ + ☐
_____
☐ + ☐ + ☐ = ☐

CHALLENGE Solve these subtraction sums on the back of the sheet.

(a) 762 – 426   (b) 927 – 282   (c) 834 – 257

Objective   *Solves subtraction sums using the expanded method.*

TEACHER INFORMATION

ADDITION AND SUBTRACTION

Objective

- Subtract numbers with up to three digits, using formal written methods of columnar subtraction.

Oral work and mental calculation

- Practise counting up from the smaller number to the larger number; for example, 605 – 596 – count up from 596 to 605 to give the answer 9.

- Use Base 10 material to illustrate subtraction with trading.

- Discuss methods for completing TU – TU sums, without and with trading. Extend to HTU – HTU sums.

- Demonstrate the column method for completing TU – TU sums. Extend this to HTU – HTU sums.

Main teaching activity

Subtraction with trading – 1 (page 51)

Additional activities suitable for developing the objective

- Transfer subtraction sums to a vertical layout; for example, change 786 – 374 = 412 to

$$\begin{array}{r} 786 \\ - \ 374 \\ \hline 412 \end{array}$$

- Practise TU - TU sums, using pencil and paper methods, without and with trading. Extend to HTU - HTU sums.

Answers

1. (a) 17   (b) 8   (c) 17   (d) 18
   (e) 438   (f) 425 (g) 629   (h) 539
   (i) 337   (j) 548

Challenge: (a) 627   (b) 523   (c) 327   (d) 228

SUBTRACTING WITH TRADING – 1

When subtracting with two or more digits, if the top number is smaller than the bottom number, we need to trade a ten from the tens column and place it in the ones column. Look at the example, 52 – 28.

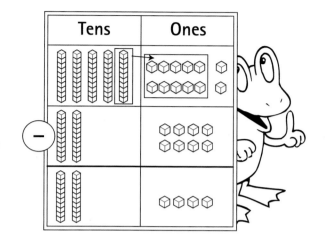

Tens	Ones

2 – 8 cannot be done. So the ones column borrows a ten (or 10 ones) from the tens column to become 12 – 8 = 4 (we can now do this sum). The tens column has now become 4 – 2 = 2

1. Subtract these numbers and remember to trade.

(a)

Tens	Ones
2	5
	8

(b)

Tens	Ones
2	2
1	4

(c)

Tens	Ones
3	5
1	8

(d)

Tens	Ones
4	6
2	8

(e)

Hundreds	Tens	Ones
6	5	4
2	1	6

(f)

Hundreds	Tens	Ones
8	6	3
4	3	8

(g)

Hundreds	Tens	Ones
9	4	8
3	1	9

(h)

Hundreds	Tens	Ones
6	7	5
1	3	6

(i)

Hundreds	Tens	Ones
5	8	4
2	4	7

(j)

Hundreds	Tens	Ones
6	8	0
1	3	2

CHALLENGE

On the back of this sheet, set these subtraction problems out vertically and solve them.

(a) 775 – 148   (b) 850 – 327   (c) 946 – 619   (d) 367 – 139

Objective   *Uses written methods to solve subtraction problems involving trading.*

TEACHER INFORMATION

ADDITION AND SUBTRACTION

Objective

- Subtract numbers with up to three digits, using formal written methods of columnar subtraction.

Oral work and mental calculation

- Practise counting up from the smaller number to the larger number; for example, 605 – 596 – count up from 596 to 605 to give the answer 9.

- Use Base 10 material to illustrate subtraction with trading.

- Discuss methods for completing TU – TU sums, without and with trading. Extend to HTU – HTU sums.

- Demonstrate the column method for completing TU – TU sums. Extend this to HTU – HTU sums.

Main teaching activity

Subtraction with trading – 2 (page 53)

Additional activities suitable for developing the objective

- Transfer subtraction sums to a vertical layout; for example, change 786 – 374 = 412 to

```
   786
 - 374
 _____
   412
 _____
```

- Practise TU - TU sums, using pencil and paper methods, without and with trading. Extend to HTU - HTU sums.

Answers

1. (a) 131   (b) 134   (c) 128   (d) 148
   (e) 226   (f) 208   (g) 495   (h) 146
   (i) 185   (j) 574   (k) 585   (l) 359

2. (a) 385   (b) 247   (c) 275   (d) 158
   (e) 343   (f) 327   (g) 383   (h) 548

Challenge: (a) 328   (b) 266   (c) 225   (d) 538

SUBTRACTING WITH TRADING – 2

1. Subtract these 3-digit numbers. Remember to start in the ones column. For some of them, you may need to trade 10 ones for 1 ten, or 10 tens for 1 hundred.

(a)

Hundreds	Tens	Ones
2	5	3
1	2	2

(b)

Hundreds	Tens	Ones
2	4	6
1	1	2

(c)

Hundreds	Tens	Ones
2	5	7
1	2	9

(d)

Hundreds	Tens	Ones
2	9	6
1	4	8

(e)

Hundreds	Tens	Ones
3	7	5
1	4	9

(f)

Hundreds	Tens	Ones
4	5	6
2	4	8

(g)

Hundreds	Tens	Ones
6	3	5
1	4	0

(h)

Hundreds	Tens	Ones
4	0	7
2	6	1

(i)

Hundreds	Tens	Ones
5	6	7
3	8	2

(j)

Hundreds	Tens	Ones
8	3	5
2	6	1

(k)

Hundreds	Tens	Ones
9	2	9
3	4	4

(l)

Hundreds	Tens	Ones
7	3	1
3	7	2

2. Solve these 3-digit subtraction problems.

(a) 745
   - 360
   _____

(b) 382
   - 135
   _____

(c) 450
   - 175
   _____

(d) 518
   - 360
   _____

(e) 639
   - 296
   _____

(f) 535
   - 208
   _____

(g) 741
   - 358
   _____

(h) 923
   - 375
   _____

CHALLENGE On the back of this sheet, set these subtraction problems out vertically and solve them.

(a) 457 – 129   (b) 506 – 240   (c) 394 – 169   (d) 924 – 386

Objective   *Uses written methods to solve subtraction problems involving trading.*

TEACHER INFORMATION

ADDITION AND SUBTRACTION

Objective

• Estimate the answer to a calculation and use inverse operations to check answers.

Oral work and mental calculation

• Without apparatus, answer oral questions; for example,

You know that 22 + 14 = 36. So, what is:
14 + 22? 36 – 22? 36 – 14?

You know that 87 – 42 = 45. So, what is:
87 – 45? 42 + 45? 45 + 42?

• Use three number cards to illustrate the fact that subtraction is the inverse of addition; for example, 25, 15 and 10.

• Use toy farm animals in the same way; for example, 3 cows + 15 cows = 18 cows, so 18 cows – 15 cows = 3 cows.

Main teaching activity

Relationship between addition and subtraction (page 55)

Additional activities suitable for developing the objective

• Complete sums with symbols standing for unknown numbers; for example, 16 + ☐ = 22, ☐ + 16 = 22, 22 – 16 = ☐, 22 - ☐ = 16

• Write two addition and subtraction sentences, using a set of three given numbers; for example, 28, 21 and 7.

Answers

1. (a) 20 – 5 = 15   (b) 19 – 17 = 2
   (c) 18 – 14 = 4   (d) 19 – 7 = 12
   (e) 18 – 11 = 7   (f) 20 – 8 = 12

2. (b) 18, 18, 3, 15   (c) 25, 25, 4, 21
   (d) 29, 29, 14, 15   (e) 30, 22, 22, 8
   (f) 32, 25, 25, 7   (g) 37, 37, 23, 14
   (h) 40, 40, 40, 40   (i) 48, 48, 26, 48
   (j) 50, 32, 18, 50

Challenge: 30 + 15 = 45, 15 + 30 = 45, 45 – 15 = 30,
              45 – 30 = 15

1. Draw a line to match the related addition and subtraction sums.

(a) 15 + 5 = 20 •   • 19 - 7 = 12

(b) 2 + 17 = 19 •   • 18 - 11 = 7

(c) 14 + 4 = 18 •   • 19 - 7 = 12

(d) 7 + 12 = 19 •   • 20 - 5 = 15

(e) 11 + 7 = 18 •   • 20 - 8 = 12

(f) 12 + 8 = 20 •   • 18 - 14 = 4

2. Fill in the missing answers for each sum below. The first one has been done for you.

Addition sum	Related addition sum	Related subtraction sum	Another related subtraction sum
(a) 16 + 4 = *20*	4 + 16 = *20*	20 - 16 = *4*	20 - 4 = *16*
(b) 15 + 3 = _____	3 + 15 = _____	18 - 15 = _____	18 - 3 = _____
(c) 21 + 4 = _____	4 + 21 = _____	25 - 21 = _____	25 - 4 = _____
(d) 14 + 15 = _____	15 + 14 = _____	29 - 15 = _____	29 - 14 = _____
(e) 22 + 8 = _____	8 + _____ = 30	30 - _____ = 8	30 - _____ = 22
(f) 25 + 7 = _____	7 + _____ = 32	32 - _____ = 7	32 - _____ = 25
(g) 23 + 14 = _____	14 + 23 = _____	37 - _____ = 14	37 - _____ = 23
(h) 22 + 18 = _____	18 + 22 = _____	_____ - 22 = 18	_____ - 18 = 22
(i) 26 + 22 = _____	22 + 26 = _____	48 - _____ = 22	_____ - 22 = 26
(j) 32 + 18 = _____	18 + _____ = 50	50 - 32 = _____	_____ - 18 = 32

CHALLENGE

Write 4 addition and subtraction number sentences using the numbers 45, 30 and 15.

_____ _____ _____ _____

Objective   *Recognises that subtraction is the inverse of addition.*

TEACHER INFORMATION

ADDITION AND SUBTRACTION

Objective

- Estimate the answer to a calculation and use inverse operations to check answers.

Oral work and mental calculation

- Give equivalent addition sums and their answers; for example, change 8 + 2 into 2 + 8. Discuss which sum is easier and why. Repeat for multiplication sums.

- Give a subtraction fact that corresponds to an addition fact; for example, 15 – 7 = 8 and 15 – 8 = 7 would correspond to 7 + 8 = 15.

- Give a division fact that corresponds to a multiplication fact; for example, 20 ÷ 4 = 5 and 20 ÷ 5 = 4 would correspond to 4 x 5 = 20.

Interactive whiteboard activity

Interactive whiteboard activity available to support this copymaster. Visit *www.prim-ed.com*.

Main teaching activity

Checking results (page 57)

Additional activities suitable for developing the objective

- Write equivalent addition sums and their answers; for example, change 10 + 5 into 5 + 10. Repeat for multiplication sums.

- Write alternative ways of writing addition sums with three numbers; for example, 5 + 7 + 9 could also be 5 + 9 + 7 or 9 + 7 + 5 or ...

- Match equivalent sums written onto cards; for example, 11 + 6 might match to 6 + 11 or 10 + 1 + 6.

- Write the corresponding addition fact to a given subtraction fact, and vice versa.

- Write the corresponding multiplication fact to a given division fact, and vice versa.

Answers

1. (a) 28, yes   (b) 29, no   (c) 34, no
    (d) 24, no   (e) 28, yes   (f) 30, no
    (g) 16, yes   (h) 50, no   (i) 30, no
    (j) 14, no

2. (a) 26, yes   (b) 30, no   (c) 34, no
    (d) 20, yes

Challenge: (a) Teacher check, yes
          (b) Teacher check, no

CHECKING RESULTS

1. Check the answers to the addition and multiplication sums by doing them in a different order. Colour to show whether the answer was correct.

(a) 10 + 18 = 28   Check: 18 + 10 = ☐   Correct? yes no

(b) 12 + 17 = 28   Check: 17 + 12 = ☐   Correct? yes no

(c) 15 + 19 = 33   Check: 19 + 15 = ☐   Correct? yes no

(d) 4 + 7 + 13 = 23   Check: 13 + 7 + 4 = ☐   Correct? yes no

(e) 8 + 16 + 4 = 28   Check: 16 + 8 + 4 = ☐   Correct? yes no

(f) 1 + 10 + 19 = 29   Check: 19 + 10 + 1 = ☐   Correct? yes no

(g) 2 x 8 = 16   Check: 8 x 2 = ☐   Correct? yes no

(h) 10 x 5 = 15   Check: 5 x 10 = ☐   Correct? yes no

(i) 5 x 6 = 35   Check: 6 x 5 = ☐   Correct? yes no

(j) 2 x 7 = 18   Check: 7 x 2 = ☐   Correct? yes no

2. Check the answers to the addition and multiplication sums by doing equivalent calculations. Colour to show whether the answer was correct.

(a) 10 + 16 = 26   Check: 10 + 10 + 6 = ☐   Correct? yes no

(b) 3 x 10 = 40   Check: 10 + 10 +10 = ☐   Correct? yes no

(c) 14 + 20 = 24   Check: 10 + 4 + 20 = ☐   Correct? yes no

(d) 4 x 5 = 20   Check: 5 + 5 + 5 + 5 = ☐   Correct? yes no

CHALLENGE Write an equivalent sum you could use and check the answer.

(a) 19 + 10 = 29   Check: _____   Correct? yes no

(b) 4 x 5 = 25   Check: _____   Correct? yes no

Objective   *Checks results of calculations with an equivalent calculation.*

TEACHER INFORMATION

ADDITION AND SUBTRACTION

Objective

- Estimate the answer to a calculation and use inverse operations to check answers.

Oral work and mental calculation

- Give equivalent addition sums; for example, 18 + 22 and 22 + 18. Discuss which sum is easier and why.

- Give equivalent multiplication sums; for example, 5 x 8 and 8 x 5. Discuss which sum is easier and why.

- Give an equivalent addition sum for a subtraction sum, and vice versa.

- Give an equivalent multiplication sum for a division sum, and vice versa.

Main teaching activity

Checking calculations (page 59)

Additional activities suitable for developing the objective

- Write as many equivalent checking sums for a given sum as they are able; for example, 8 x 4 = 32

- Write alternative ways of writing addition/ multiplication sums with three numbers; for example, 5 + 6 + 7 could also be 6 + 7 + 5 or ...?

- Match equivalent sums written onto cards; for example, 3 x 4 might match to 12 ÷ 4.

- Play 'Equivalent bingo' with the above cards.

Answers

1. (a) 15, yes   (b) 70, no   (c) 3, yes   (d) 20, no

2. (a) 31, no   (b) 55, yes   (c) 50, yes   (d) 27, no

3. (a) 6 + 6 + 6 = 18 and 18 - 12 = 6
    (b) 25 + 35 = 60 and 60 – 35 = 25
    (c) 5 x 8 = 40, 8 + 8 + 8 + 8 + 8 = 40 and 40 ÷ 5 = 8
    (d) 24 ÷ 6 = 4 and 4 x 6 = 24

Challenge: (a) Teacher check, yes
                   (b) Teacher check, yes

CHECKING CALCULATIONS

1. Check the answers to the sums by using a different operation. Colour to show whether the answer was correct.

    (a) 10 + 15 = 25   Check: 25 - 10 = ☐   Correct? yes | no

    (b) 80 - 30 = 40   Check: 30 + 40 = ☐   Correct? yes | no

    (c) 3 x 4 = 12   Check: 12 ÷ 4 = ☐   Correct? yes | no

    (d) 25 ÷ 5 = 4   Check: 5 x 4 = ☐   Correct? yes | no

2. Check the answers to the addition and multiplication sums by doing them in a different order. Colour to show whether the answer was correct.

    (a) 15 + 16 = 30   Check: 16 + 15 = ☐   Correct? yes | no

    (b) 20 + 35 = 55   Check: 35 + 20 = ☐   Correct? yes | no

    (c) 10 x 5 = 50   Check: 5 x 10 = ☐   Correct? yes | no

    (d) 9 x 3 = 28   Check: 3 x 9 = ☐   Correct? yes | no

3. Tick the sums that can be used to check the given calculations.

    (a) 6 + 12 = 18

| ☐ 6 + 6 + 6 = 18 | ☐ 18 + 6 = 12 | ☐ 18 - 12 = 6 |

    (b) 60 - 25 = 35

| ☐ 60 + 35 = 25 | ☐ 25 + 35 = 60 | ☐ 60 - 35 = 25 |

    (c) 8 x 5 = 40

| ☐ 5 x 8 = 40 | ☐ 8 + 8 + 8 + 8 + 8 = 40 | ☐ 40 ÷ 5 = 8 |

    (d) 24 ÷ 4 = 6

| ☐ 24 ÷ 6 = 4 | ☐ 4 x 6 = 24 | ☐ 6 ÷ 4 = 24 |

CHALLENGE For the following sums, write a sum you could use to check each answer, mentioning if the sum is correct or not. Use the back of this sheet.
(a) 19 + 17 = 36   (b) 30 ÷ 5 = 6

Objective   *Uses a range of methods to check calculations.*

TEACHER INFORMATION

ADDITION AND SUBTRACTION

Objective

- Solve problems, including missing number problems, using number facts.

Oral work and mental calculation

- Respond rapidly to oral questions; for example, $6 + 2 = ?$, $5 + ? = 12$, $19 - ? = 15$, $20 - ? = 4$.

- Work out the missing symbol in sums; for example, $6 ? 8 = 14$, $20 ? 10 = 10$.

Interactive whiteboard activity

Interactive whiteboard activity available to support this copymaster. Visit *www.prim-ed.com*.

Main teaching activity

Unknown symbols and numbers (page 61)

Additional activities suitable for developing the objective

- Record sums using the symbols +, – and =.

- Complete an +/– sum with a symbol representing a missing number; for example,

  $6 + 2 = \square$ $5 + \square = 15$ $\square - \triangle = 12$

- Make up number stories to reflect statements; for example, $\square - 2 = 19$.

- Fill in missing signs in sums; for example, $5 \square 15 = 20$.

Answers

1. (a) +   (b) –   (c) +   (d) +
   (e) –   (f) +   (g) –   (h) –
   (i) +   (j) +   (k) +   (l) –

2. (a) 9   (b) 12   (c) 10   (d) 14
   (e) 9   (f) 14   (g) 7   (h) 6
   (i) 20   (j) 29   (k) 24   (l) 30

3. (a) 8   (b) +   (c) +   (d) 10
   (e) –   (f) –   (g) 20   (h) –
   (i) 9   (j) 8   (k) 11   (l) 14

Challenge: Teacher check

UNKNOWN SYMBOLS AND NUMBERS

1. Write the symbol + or − into the box to complete each sum.

(a) 8 ☐ 7 = 15   (b) 10 ☐ 3 = 7   (c) 10 ☐ 2 = 12

(d) 2 ☐ 4 = 6   (e) 20 ☐ 10 = 10   (f) 15 ☐ 12 = 27

(g) 19 ☐ 12 = 7   (h) 5 ☐ 5 = 0   (i) 6 ☐ 2 = 8

(j) 20 ☐ 16 = 36   (k) 14 ☐ 2 = 16   (l) 39 ☐ 16 = 23

2. Write the missing number into the box to complete each addition and subtraction sum.

(a) 5 + ☐ = 14   (b) 10 + ☐ = 22

(c) 16 + ☐ = 26   (d) ☐ + 20 = 34

(e) ☐ + 9 = 18   (f) ☐ + 22 = 36

(g) 10 − ☐ = 3   (h) 19 − ☐ = 13

(i) 43 − ☐ = 23   (j) ☐ − 10 = 19

(k) ☐ − 20 = 4   (l) ☐ − 15 = 15

3. Write the missing number or symbol into the box to complete each addition and subtraction sum.

(a) 3 + 5 = ☐   (b) 6 ☐ 10 = 16   (c) 3 ☐ 3 = 6

(d) 9 + ☐ = 19   (e) 16 ☐ 2 = 14   (f) 25 ☐ 5 = 20

(g) 25 − 5 = ☐   (h) 70 ☐ 10 = 60   (i) 90 + ☐ = 99

(j) 16 − ☐ = 8   (k) ☐ − 5 = 6   (l) ☐ + 2 = 16

CHALLENGE Write the missing numbers into each sum.

(a) ☐ + △ = 10
△ + ☐ = 10

(b) ☐ − △ = 10
△ − ☐ = 10

Objective *Recognises the use of a symbol to stand for an unknown number or operation.*

TEACHER INFORMATION

ADDITION AND SUBTRACTION

Objective

- Solve problems, including missing number problems, using number facts.

Oral work and mental calculation

- Work out simple one-step problems with the class as an oral activity; for example, If 12 adults and 4 children went on a picnic, how many people went altogether? If there were 16 ice-creams and 5 melted, how many ice-creams were left?

- Work out money problems with the class as an oral activity; for example,
  - I have £15. I am given another £4. How much money do I have altogether?
  - Amy bought four sweets at 10p each. How much did she spend altogether? How much change did she receive from 50p?
  - You have three silver coins in your purse. What coins could you have? What totals might these coins give?

- Use the class shop to add up simple shopping totals and work out simple amounts of change.

- Work out measures problems with the class as an oral activity; for example,
  - Jess is 140 cm tall. Bill is 135 cm tall. How much taller is Jess?
  - Ahmed went into a shop at 11.20 a.m. He came out at 11.35 a.m. How long was he in the shop?

- Verbalise how problems are solved.

Interactive whiteboard activity

Interactive whiteboard activity available to support this copymaster. Visit *www.prim-ed.com*.

Main teaching activity

'Real life' problems (page 63)

Additional activities suitable for developing the objective

- Introduce two-step operations for working out problems; for example,
  Make a transport game with the pupils all taking part:
  The bus leaves with 3 people on board. It stops at the post office and two ladies get on. Then it travels to the library and one person gets off. Two gentlemen get on ... and so on.

- Make some cakes and price them. Ask a pupil to come and buy 3 cakes at 5p each and one slice of cake for 10p. How much would the pupil have to pay?

- Make a class day-diary. Work out the times the children get up and the time they leave for school – how long did it take them to get ready?

Answers

1. (a) £12 + £8 = £20
   (b) 98p – 45p = 53p
   (c) 95 kg – 12 kg = 83 kg
   (d) 50 kg + 49 kg = 99 kg
   (e) 94 – 83 = 11
   (f) 90 cm + 80 cm = 170 cm

Challenge: 12 + 8 – 5 = 15

'REAL LIFE' PROBLEMS

1. Use + or – to solve these word problems. Explain how each problem was solved.

Problem	Number sentence	How I solved the problem
(a) Kelly has £12 and Laura has £8. How much money do they have altogether?	☐ ☐ ☐ = ☐	
(b) Belinda had 98p. She spent 45p on a drink. How much change did she receive?	☐ ☐ ☐ = ☐	
(c) John weighed 95 kg. He went on a diet and lost 12 kg. How much does he now weigh?	☐ ☐ ☐ = ☐	
(d) Abdul weighs 50 kg and Anna weighs 49 kg. What is their combined weight?	☐ ☐ ☐ = ☐	
(e) Ben ran a race in 83 seconds. Sam ran the same race in 94 seconds. How many seconds faster was Ben?	☐ ☐ ☐ = ☐	
(f) Ainsley has a 90 cm length of liquorice. Dario has an 80 cm length. How long would their liquorice be if placed end to end?	☐ ☐ ☐ = ☐	

CHALLENGE

Solve this problem using +, –, x or ÷. Complete the number sentence.

12 people are on a bus. 8 more get on and 5 get off. How many people are on the bus now?

☐ ☐ ☐ ☐ ☐ = ☐

Objective *Solves word problems involving missing numbers and explains how problems are solved.*

TEACHER INFORMATION

ADDITION AND SUBTRACTION

Objective

- Solve problems using number facts.

Oral work and mental calculation

- Use the appropriate vocabulary: *operation*, *sign*, *symbol*, *number sentence* and *equation*.

- Give the class a word problem. Ask them whether it needs addition, subtraction, multiplication or division to solve the word problem. Discuss how they know.

- Work out the answer to the word problem. Discuss how to best work it out. Can it be worked out mentally or do they need to work it out on paper? Do the pupils need apparatus to help work it out; for example, a number line, cubes or coins?

- Give pupils a simple addition statement; for example, 25 + 34. Ask pupils to make up a word problem that reflects this addition statement.

Main teaching activity

Addition word problems (page 65)

Additional activities suitable for developing the objective

- Work out word problems and write the answer in a number sentence; for example,

  A pencil costs 54p, a notebook 99p and an eraser 42p. How much does the stationery cost altogether?

- Give pupils a simple addition statement; for example, 25 + 34. Ask pupils to write a word problem that reflects this addition statement.

- Write the unknown operation sign into number sentences; for example, 63 ? 24 = 87.

Answers

1. (a) 5 + 8 = 13   (b) 14 + 23 = 37
    (c) 37 + 29 = 66   (d) 25 + 17 = 42
    (e) 19 + 15 = 34   (f) 3 + 5 + 2 + 6 = 16

2. (a) 14 + 8 = 22, Teacher check
    (b) 54 + 32 = 86, Teacher check

Challenge: Teacher check

ADDITION WORD PROBLEMS

1. Read, set out and solve these addition word problems.

(a) Jacob travels 5 km to school and Fergus travels 8 km. How many kilometres do they travel altogether?		*5 + 8 =* _____
(b) There were 14 pieces of fruit in one bowl and 23 pieces in another bowl. How many pieces of fruit altogether?		*14* *+ 23* _____
(c) One rose bush has 37 flowers and another has 29 flowers. How many flowers altogether?		
(d) There are 25 books on one shelf and 17 books on another. How many books altogether?		
(e) If Sarah has 19 stickers and Liana has 15, how many stickers do they have altogether?		
(f) There are 4 cats which had kittens. The first had 3, the second had 5, the third had 2 and the fourth had 6. How many kittens altogether?		

2. Write your own addition word problems for these sums.

(a) 14 + 8 = _____

(b) 54 + 32 = _____

CHALLENGE Check your answers. Tick (✔) them if they are correct and cross (✗) them if they are incorrect. Redo the incorrect sums on the back of the sheet.

Objective   *Selects appropriate methods to solve word problems involving addition of whole numbers.*

TEACHER INFORMATION

ADDITION AND SUBTRACTION

Objective

- Solve problems using number facts.

Oral work and mental calculation

- Use the appropriate vocabulary: *operation*, *sign*, *symbol*, *number sentence* and *equation*.

- Give the class a word problem. Ask them whether it needs addition, subtraction, multiplication or division to solve the word problem. Discuss how they know.

- Work out the answer to the word problem. Discuss how to best work it out. Can it be worked out mentally or do they need to work it out on paper? Do the pupils need apparatus to help work it out; for example, a number line, cubes or coins?

- Give pupils a simple subtraction statement; for example, 69 – 27. Ask pupils to make up a word problem that reflects this subtraction statement.

Main teaching activity

Subtraction word problems (page 67)

Additional activities suitable for developing the objective

- Work out word problems and write the answer in a number sentence; for example,

  Julie has a £5 note. She spends £3.50 at the shop. How much change should she receive?

- Give pupils a simple subtraction statement; for example, 87 – 23. Ask pupils to write a word problem that reflects this subtraction statement.

- Write the unknown operation sign into number sentences; for example, 90 ? 45 = 45.

Answers

1. (a) 16 – 4 = 12   (b) 45 – 28 = 17
   (c) 158 – 123 = 35   (d) 75 – 48 = 27
   (e) 20 – 8 = 12   (f) 278 – 140 = 138

2. (a) 15 – 7 = 8, Teacher check
   (b) 42 – 27 = 15, Teacher check

Challenge: Teacher check

SUBTRACTION WORD PROBLEMS

1. Read, set out and solve these subtraction word problems.

(a) Ben had 16 cars until he gave his friend 4 of them. How many cars did he have left?		*16 - 4 =* _____
(b) There were 45 litres of water in the farm water tank. If the farmer used 28 litres to water the corn, how much water was left?		$\begin{array}{r} 45 \\ -\ 28 \\ \hline \end{array}$
(c) 158 litres of petrol were pumped into the truck. If 123 litres were used on a journey, how much petrol was left?		
(d) There were 75 apples on the tree. If 48 were picked, how many apples were left?		
(e) Liam had 20 balloons at his party. If he gave away 8 to his friends, how many balloons did he have left?		
(f) There are 278 pages in a novel. If Dad has read 140 pages, how many more pages does he have left to read?		

2. Write your own subtraction word problems for the following.

(a) 15 – 7 = _____

(b) 42 – 27 = _____

CHALLENGE Check your answers. Tick (✔) them if they are correct and cross (✗) them if they are incorrect. Redo the incorrect sums on the back of the sheet.

Objective *Selects appropriate methods to solve word problems involving subtraction of whole numbers.*

TEACHER INFORMATION

ADDITION AND SUBTRACTION

Objective

- Solve problems, including using number facts and place value.

Oral work and mental calculation

- Hold up a card with a three-digit number on it. Ask the class questions such as, 'What number is on this card?', 'Point to the ten' and 'What number is the unit?'

- Hang a series of three-digit numbers on the class washing line. Give the pupils instructions, such as, 'Go and fetch me the number 56'.

- Say what the digits in three-digit numbers represent; for example, the 4 in 465 represents 400 (or 4 hundreds), the 6 in 65 represents 60 (or 6 tens) and the 5 represents 5 (or 5 ones).

- State the number that is equivalent to 5 hundreds, 7 tens and 4 ones (574).

Main teaching activity

Addition and subtraction patterns (page 69)

Additional activities suitable for developing the objective

- Explore Hundreds, Tens and Units/Ones and what each figure in a three-digit number represents.

- Play a matching game of numbers in digits and words. Shuffle the cards well to begin the game.

- Expand numbers; for example, 248 is 200 + 40 + 8. Show the number on an abacus.

- Complete HTU sums using unknown numbers; for example,

  125 = 100 + _____ + 5 or 736 = 700 + 30 + _____

- Use money to explain Tens and Units/Ones; for example, give me 68p in tens and ones or change twenty-two pennies for two tens and two pennies.

Answers

1. (a) 9, 90 (b) 22, 170 + 50 = 220
   (c) 6, 80 − 20 = 60 (d) 12, 180 − 60 = 120

2. (a) 80 (b) 70 + 80 = 150
   (c) 90 + 20 = 110 (d) 50 + 60 = 110
   (e) 40 + 30 = 70 (f) 80 + 90 = 170

3. (a) 40 (b) 70 − 30 = 40
   (c) 90 − 40 = 50 (d) 100 − 60 = 40
   (e) 120 − 50 = 70 (f) 150 − 70 = 80

Challenge: (a) 200 (b) 210 (c) 240

ADDITION AND SUBTRACTION PATTERNS

1. Answer and extend these addition and subtraction sums by adding a zero to the numbers; e.g. 5 + 4 = 9, 50 + 40 = 90.

   (a) 3 + 6 = _____   30 + 60 = _____

   (b) 17 + 5 = _____   _____ + _____ = _____

   (c) 8 - 2 = _____   _____ - _____ = _____

   (d) 18 - 6 = _____   _____ - _____ = _____

2. Write and solve the addition number sentence to match the picture.

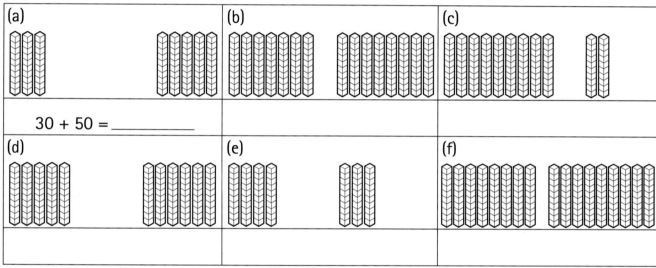

(a)	(b)	(c)
30 + 50 = _____		
(d)	(e)	(f)

3. Write and solve the subtraction number sentence to match the picture.

(a)	(b)	(c)
60 - 20 = _____		
(d)	(e)	(f)

CHALLENGE   Solve these extended multiplication problems.

(a) 40 x 5 = _____   (b) 70 x 3 = _____   (c) 4 x 60 = _____

Objective   *Solves maths problems by recognising simple patterns and relationships.*

TEACHER INFORMATION

ADDITION AND SUBTRACTION

Objective

- Solve problems, including missing number problems, using number facts and more complex addition.

Oral work and mental calculation

- Demonstrate that addition can be done in any order to do mental calculations more efficiently; for example, put the largest number first and count on.

- Mentally add three or more small numbers between 1 and 20. Extend to 50.

- Respond to questions; for example, What is 9 plus 3 plus 2? Add 16 and 5 and 4. Tell me three numbers that add up to 20.

Interactive whiteboard activity

Interactive whiteboard activity available to support this copymaster. Visit *www.prim-ed.com.*

Main teaching activity

Adding more than two numbers (page 71)

Additional activities suitable for developing the objective

- Use number lines and number squares to explore three hops; for example, 40 + ___ + ___ = 100

- Find all the different totals you can make by using three of these five numbers; for example, 20, 15, 32, 43, 8.

- Choose three items from a retail catalogue. Total the cost.

- Measure the heights of three pupils. Total the heights.

Answers

1. (a) 16   (b) 15   (c) 16   (d) 18
   (e) 22   (f) 22

2. Answers will vary

3. (a) 67   (b) 99   (c) 69   (d) 87
   (e) 87   (f) 98   (g) 89   (h) 88

4. Answers will vary

Challenge: 22 blocks

ADDING MORE THAN TWO NUMBERS

1. Solve these addition sums.

(a)   5
      4
    + 7
   _____

   _____

(b)   7
      6
    + 2
   _____

   _____

(c)   4
      5
    + 7
   _____

   _____

(d)   6
      3
      4
    + 5
   _____

   _____

(e)   8
      2
      5
    + 7
   _____

   _____

(f)   3
      9
      6
    + 4
   _____

   _____

2. Use three numbers to complete these sums.

(a) [4] + [   ] + [   ] = 10

(b) [5] + [   ] + [   ] = 10

(c) [9] + [   ] + [   ] = 20

(d) [8] + [   ] + [   ] = 20

3. Solve these addition sums.

(a)   12
      20
    + 35
   _____

   _____

(b)   23
      45
    + 31
   _____

   _____

(c)   30
      24
    + 15
   _____

   _____

(d)   14
      50
    + 23
   _____

   _____

(e)   31
      20
      14
    + 22
   _____

   _____

(f)   23
      51
      10
    + 14
   _____

   _____

(g)   35
      20
      11
    + 23
   _____

   _____

(h)   12
      21
      33
    + 22
   _____

   _____

4. Use three numbers to complete these sums.

(a) [25] + [   ] + [   ] = 50

(b) [20] + [   ] + [   ] = 50

CHALLENGE

There are eight red, seven blue, two yellow and five green
blocks in the box. How many blocks are there altogether?
(You may wish to set out the sum on the back of this sheet.)

[   ]

blocks

Objective   *Adds 3–4 one- and two-digit numbers.*

TEACHER INFORMATION

ADDITION AND SUBTRACTION

Objective

- Solve problems using number facts and more complex addition and subtraction.

Oral work and mental calculation

- Use the appropriate vocabulary: *operation*, *sign*, *symbol*, *number sentence* and *equation*.

- Give the class a word problem. Ask them whether it needs addition, subtraction, multiplication or division to solve the word problem. Discuss how they know.

- Work out the answer to the word problem. Discuss how to best work it out. Can it be worked out mentally or do they need to work it out on paper? Do the pupils need apparatus to help work it out; for example, a number line, cubes or coins?

- Give pupils a simple +/- statement. Ask pupils to make up a word problem that reflects this +/- statement.

Interactive whiteboard activity

Interactive whiteboard activity available to support this copymaster. Visit *www.prim-ed.com*.

Main teaching activity

Addition and subtraction word problems (page 73)

Additional activities suitable for developing the objective

- Work out word problems and write the answer in a number sentence.

- Give pupils a simple +/- statement. Ask pupils to write a word problem that reflects this +/- statement.

- Write the unknown operation sign into number sentences.

Answers

1. (a) add, mentally, 5 + 5 + 5 + 5 = 20 eggs
   (b) add, written,
       578 + 231 + 405 = 1214 people
   (c) subtract, mentally, 15 m – 3 m – 2 m = 10 m
   (d) subtract, written,
       £2.50 – 55p – 60p = £1.35
   (e) add, written,
       19 + 19 + 19 = 57 cans
   (f) add, written,
       97 km + 64 km + 56 km = 217 km

Challenge: (a) 165 + 250 + 121 = 536
             (b) 72 – 36 – 25 = 11

ADDITION AND SUBTRACTION WORD PROBLEMS

1. Read the problem, circle the process and the method you will use to solve it. Show your workings and answer.

Word problem	Process	Method	Workings and answer
(a) 4 chickens in the hen house each laid 5 eggs in a week. How many eggs altogether?	Add Subtract	Mentally Written	
(b) 578 people live in Lakeside, 231 live in Rivervale and 405 live in Brookville. How many people altogether?	Add Subtract	Mentally Written	
(c) Sophie had a 15 m piece of string. Her dog chewed off 3 m, and she gave 2 m to a friend. How much string does Sophie have left?	Add Subtract	Mentally Written	
(d) Lisa had £2.50. She spent 55p on a packet of crisps and 60p on a cookie. How much money did she have left?	Add Subtract	Mentally Written	
(e) At the supermarket there were 3 boxes with 19 cans of soup in each box. How many cans altogether?	Add Subtract	Mentally Written	
(f) The Brooks family drove 97 km on Saturday, 64 km on Sunday and 56 km on Monday. How many kilometres did they travel altogether?	Add Subtract	Mentally Written	

CHALLENGE

On the back of this sheet, write your own word problems for these.

(a) 165 + 250 + 121 = _____   (b) 72 – 36 – 25 = _____

Objective   *Selects appropriate operations and methods to solve word problems involving whole numbers.*

TEACHER INFORMATION

MULTIPLICATION AND DIVISION

Objective

*   Recall and use multiplication facts for the 3 multiplication table.

Oral work and mental calculation

*   Chant the three times table – forwards and backwards.

*   Respond quickly to oral questions phrased in a variety of ways; for example, Six threes, 3 times 3, 5 multiplied by 3, Multiply 4 by 3, How many threes in 21?, Divide 24 by 3.

*   Play 'Tables knockout'. All pupils stand in a circle. Pair up pupils and ask them a question from the three times table. The pupil who answers correctly remains standing. The other pupil sits down. The winner is the last pupil left standing.

Main teaching activity

Multiplying by three (page 75)

Additional activities suitable for developing the objective

*   Play 'Tables dominoes' and 'Tables bingo'.

*   Play 'Maths snap', using cards made with the x3 multiplication facts and the related division facts.

*   Give division facts (÷3) and time how long it takes for pupils to write the related multiplication facts.

Answers

1. (a) 12   (b) 24   (c) 99

2. (a) $3 \times 2 = 6$ (b) $3 \times 4 = 12$
    (c) $3 \times 3 = 9$ (d) $3 \times 8 = 24$

3. (a) 3   (b) 6   (c) 9   (d) 12
    (e) 15   (f) 18   (g) 21   (h) 24
    (i) 27   (j) 30

4. (a) 3   (b) 6   (c) 9   (d) 4, 12
    (e) 5, 15   (f) 6, 18   (g) 3, 7, 21   (h) 3, 8, 24
    (i) 3, 9, 27   (j) 3, 10, 30

Challenge: 3, 6, 9, 2, 5, 8, 1, 4, 7, 0

MULTIPLYING BY THREE

1	2	3	4	5	6	7	8	9	10
11	12	13	14	15	16	17	18	19	20
21	22	23	24	25	26	27	28	29	30
31	32	33	34	35	36	37	38	39	40
41	42	43	44	45	46	47	48	49	50
51	52	53	54	55	56	57	58	59	60
61	62	63	64	65	66	67	68	69	70
71	72	73	74	75	76	77	78	79	80
81	82	83	84	85	86	87	88	89	90
91	92	93	94	95	96	97	98	99	100

1. Count and colour in 3s on the hundreds chart.

   (a) The fourth number coloured is

   _____.

   (b) The 8th number

   coloured is _____.

   (c) The last number

   coloured is _____.

2. Complete the number sentences.

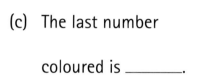

(a)	(b)	(c)	(d)
3 x _2_ = _____	3 x _____ = _____	3 x _____ = _____	3 x _____ = _____

3. Fill in the 3 times table below.

   (a) 1 x 3 = _____   (b) 2 x 3 = _____   (c) 3 x 3 = _____   (d) 4 x 3 = _____

   (e) 5 x 3 = _____   (f) 6 x 3 = _____   (g) 7 x 3 = _____   (h) 8 x 3 = _____

   (i) 9 x 3 = _____   (j) 10 x 3 = _____

4. Complete the pattern of these number sentences using the 3 times table.

   (a) 3 x 1 = _____   (b) 3 x 2 = _____   (c) 3 x 3 = _____   (d) 3 x _____ = _____

   (e) 3 x _____ = _____   (f) 3 x _____ = _____   (g) _____ x _____ = _____

   (h) _____ x _____ = _____   (i) _____ x _____ = _____   (j) _____ x _____ = _____

CHALLENGE

What constant pattern can you see appearing in the answers of the 3 times table?

_____

Objective *Recalls multiplication facts of the 3 times table.*

TEACHER INFORMATION

MULTIPLICATION AND DIVISION

Objective

- Recall and use multiplication facts for the 4 multiplication table.

Oral work and mental calculation

- Chant the four times table – forwards and backwards.

- Respond quickly to oral questions phrased in a variety of ways; for example, Six fours, 3 times 4, 5 multiplied by 4, Multiply 4 by 4, How many fours in 28?, Divide 24 by 4.

- Play 'Tables knockout'. All pupils stand in a circle. Pair up pupils and ask them a question from the four times table. The pupil who answers correctly remains standing. The other pupil sits down. The winner is the last pupil left standing.

Main teaching activity

Multiplying by four (page 77)

Additional activities suitable for developing the objective

- Play 'Tables dominoes' and 'Tables bingo'.

- Play 'Maths snap', using cards made with the x4 multiplication facts and the related division facts.

- Give division facts (÷4) and time how long it takes for pupils to write the related multiplication facts.

Answers

1. (a) even   (b) 20   (c) 48   (d) 100

2. (a) 4 x 4 = 16   (b) 4 x 6 = 24
   (c) 4 x 8 = 32   (d) 4 x 5 = 20

3. (a) 4   (b) 8   (c) 12   (d) 16
   (e) 20   (f) 24   (g) 28   (h) 32
   (i) 36   (j) 40

4. (a) 4   (b) 8   (c) 12   (d) 4, 16
   (e) 5, 20   (f) 6, 24   (g) 4, 7, 28   (h) 4, 8, 32
   (i) 4, 9, 36   (j) 4, 10, 40

Challenge: 4, 8, 2, 6, 0

MULTIPLYING BY FOUR

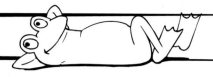

1. Count and colour in 4s on the hundreds chart.

   (a) The numbers coloured are also called

   _____ numbers.

   (b) The 5th number coloured is _____.

   (c) The 12th number coloured is _____.

   (d) The last number coloured is _____.

1	2	3	4	5	6	7	8	9	10
11	12	13	14	15	16	17	18	19	20
21	22	23	24	25	26	27	28	29	30
31	32	33	34	35	36	37	38	39	40
41	42	43	44	45	46	47	48	49	50
51	52	53	54	55	56	57	58	59	60
61	62	63	64	65	66	67	68	69	70
71	72	73	74	75	76	77	78	79	80
81	82	83	84	85	86	87	88	89	90
91	92	93	94	95	96	97	98	99	100

2. Complete the number sentences.

(a)	(b)	(c)	(d)
4 x _4_ = _____	4 x _____ = _____	4 x _____ = _____	4 x _____ = _____

3. Fill in the 4 times table below.

   (a) 1 x 4 = _____   (b) 2 x 4 = _____   (c) 3 x 4 = _____   (d) 4 x 4 = _____

   (e) 5 x 4 = _____   (f) 6 x 4 = _____   (g) 7 x 4 = _____   (h) 8 x 4 = _____

   (i) 9 x 4 = _____   (j) 10 x 4 = _____

4. Complete the pattern of these number sentences using the 4 times table.

   (a) 4 x 1 = _____   (b) 4 x 2 = _____   (c) 4 x 3 = _____   (d) 4 x _____ = _____

   (e) 4 x _____ = _____   (f) 4 x _____ = _____   (g) _____ x _____ = _____

   (h) _____ x _____ = _____   (i) _____ x _____ = _____   (j) _____ x _____ = _____

CHALLENGE

What constant pattern can you see appearing in the answers of the 4 times table?

_____

_____

Objective   *Recalls multiplication facts of the 4 times table.*

TEACHER INFORMATION

MULTIPLICATION AND DIVISION

Objective

• Recall and use multiplication facts for the 8 multiplication table.

Oral work and mental calculation

• Chant the eight times table – forwards and backwards.

• Respond quickly to oral questions phrased in a variety of ways; for example, Six eights, 3 times 8, 5 multiplied by 8, Multiply 4 by 8, How many eights in 24?, Divide 24 by 8.

• Play 'Tables knockout'. All pupils stand in a circle. Pair up pupils and ask them a question from the eight times table. The pupil who answers correctly remains standing. The other pupil sits down. The winner is the last pupil left standing.

Main teaching activity

Multiplying by eight (page 79)

Additional activities suitable for developing the objective

• Play 'Tables dominoes' and 'Tables bingo'.

• Play 'Maths snap', using cards made with the x8 multiplication facts and the related division facts.

• Give division facts (÷8) and time how long it takes for pupils to write the related multiplication facts.

Answers

1. (a) 32   (b) 64   (c) 96

2. (a) 8 x 2 = 16   (b) 8 x 4 = 32
    (c) 8 x 3 = 24   (d) 8 x 8 = 64

3. (a) 8   (b) 16   (c) 24   (d) 32
    (e) 40   (f) 48   (g) 56   (h) 64
    (i) 72   (j) 80

4. (a) 8   (b) 16   (c) 24   (d) 4, 32
    (e) 5, 40   (f) 6, 48   (g) 8, 7, 56   (h) 8, 8, 64
    (i) 8, 9, 72   (j) 8, 10, 80

Challenge: 8, 6, 4, 2, 0

MULTIPLYING BY EIGHT

1	2	3	4	5	6	7	8	9	10
11	12	13	14	15	16	17	18	19	20
21	22	23	24	25	26	27	28	29	30
31	32	33	34	35	36	37	38	39	40
41	42	43	44	45	46	47	48	49	50
51	52	53	54	55	56	57	58	59	60
61	62	63	64	65	66	67	68	69	70
71	72	73	74	75	76	77	78	79	80
81	82	83	84	85	86	87	88	89	90
91	92	93	94	95	96	97	98	99	100

1. Count and colour in 8s on the hundreds chart.

   (a) The fourth number coloured is

   _____.

   (b) The 8th number

   coloured is _____.

   (c) The last number

   coloured is _____.

2. Complete the number sentences.

(a)	(b)	(c)	(d)
8 x _2_ = _____	8 x _____ = _____	8 x _____ = _____	8 x _____ = _____

3. Fill in the 8 times table below.

   (a) 1 x 8 = _____   (b) 2 x 8 = _____   (c) 3 x 8 = _____   (d) 4 x 8 = _____

   (e) 5 x 8 = _____   (f) 6 x 8 = _____   (g) 7 x 8 = _____   (h) 8 x 8 = _____

   (i) 9 x 8 = _____   (j) 10 x 8 = _____

4. Complete the pattern of these number sentences using the 8 times table.

   (a) 8 x 1 = _____   (b) 8 x 2 = _____   (c) 8 x 3 = _____   (d) 8 x _____ = _____

   (e) 8 x _____ = _____   (f) 8 x _____ = _____   (g) _____ x _____ = _____

   (h) _____ x _____ = _____   (i) _____ x _____ = _____   (j) _____ x _____ = _____

CHALLENGE

What constant pattern can you see appearing in the answers of the 8 times table?

_____

Objective   *Recalls multiplication facts of the 8 times table.*

TEACHER INFORMATION

MULTIPLICATION AND DIVISION

Objective

* Recall and use multiplication facts for the 3, 4 and 8 multiplication tables.

Oral work and mental calculation

* Chant the 3, 4 and 8 times tables – forwards and backwards.

* Respond quickly to oral questions phrased in a variety of ways; for example, Four twos, 3 times 4, 5 multiplied by 8, Multiply 4 by 5, How many eights in 80?, Divide 24 by 4.

* Play 'Tables knockout'. All pupils stand in a circle. Pair up pupils and ask them a question from the 3, 4 and 8 times tables. The pupil who answers correctly remains standing. The other pupil sits down. The winner is the last pupil left standing.

Interactive whiteboard activity

Interactive whiteboard activity available to support this copymaster. Visit *www.prim-ed.com*.

Main teaching activity

Multiplication facts (page 81)

Additional activities suitable for developing the objective

* Play 'Tables dominoes' and 'Tables bingo'.

* Play 'Maths snap', using cards made with 3, 4 and 8 multiplication facts and the related division facts.

* Give division facts (÷ 3, 4 and 8) and time how long it takes for pupils to write the related multiplication facts.

Answers

1. Teacher check
   (a) 4, 8, 12, 16, 20   (b) 8, 16, 24, 32, 40

2. (a) 12, 3, 18, 27, 21, 6   (b) 32, 20, 4, 16, 36, 8
   (c) 24, 8, 64, 56, 80, 40

3. (a) 20   (b) 21   (c) 16   (d) 48
   (e) 9   (f) 36   (g) 80   (h) 28
   (i) 4   (j) 3   (k) 4   (l) 8

Challenge: Teacher check

MULTIPLICATION FACTS

1. Complete the multiplication table.

X	1	2	3	4	5	6	7	8	9	10
2										
3										
4										
5										
8										
10										

(a) What same answers appear in the 2 and 4 times tables?

_____

_____

(b) What same answers appear in the 4 and 8 times tables?

_____

_____

2. Complete these multiplication wheels.

(a)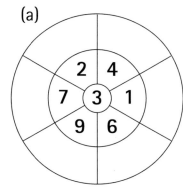

(b)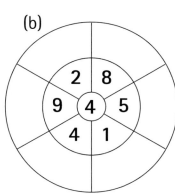

(c)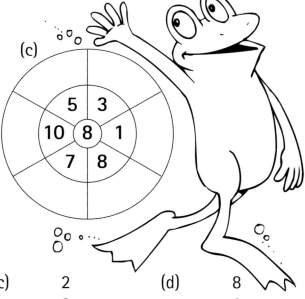

3. Answer these multiplication problems.

(a)   5
    x 4
    _____

    _____

(b)   7
    x 3
    _____

    _____

(c)   2
    x 8
    _____

    _____

(d)   8
    x 6
    _____

    _____

(e) 3 x 3 = _____

(f) 9 x 4 = _____

(g) 10 x 8 = _____

(h) 7 x 4 = _____

(i) 6 x _____ = 24

(j) 9 x _____ = 27

(k) _____ x 5 = 20

(l) 8 x _____ = 64

CHALLENGE

Take turns with a partner to ask each other a 3, 4 and 8 times table problem/question.

Objective   *Recalls multiplication facts of the 3, 4 and 8 times tables.*

TEACHER INFORMATION

MULTIPLICATION AND DIVISION

Objective

- Recall and use division facts for the 3, 4 and 8 multiplication tables.

Oral work and mental calculation

- Use the vocabulary: *divide*, *share* and *halve*.

- Complete practical sharing and grouping tasks, verbalising actions; for example,

  Sharing: 6 apples are shared between 3 horses. How many apples does each horse get?

  Grouping: There are 20 sweets in a jar. How many bags of 4 sweets can be made?

- Solve division calculations by using multiplication strategies; for example,

  Calculate 15 ÷ 3 by counting how many jumps of 3 are needed on a number line to reach 15.

- Respond rapidly to oral questions phrased in a variety of ways; for example,

  Share 15 between 3, How many eights make 64?, Divide 24 by 4, Is 21 a multiple of 3?

Interactive whiteboard activity

Interactive whiteboard activity available to support this copymaster. Visit *www.prim-ed.com*.

Main teaching activity

Sharing (page 83)

Additional activities suitable for developing the objective

- Solve division word problems; for example,

  A baker bakes 24 buns. 3 buns are put into each box. How many boxes will the baker need?

  Ainsley has used 12 tiles to make a pattern. One tile in every four is red. How many tiles are red?

- Use counters or a number line to work out the unknown numbers; for example,

  16 ÷ 4 = ___, 24 ÷ ___ = 3, ___ ÷ 3 = 8

Answers

1. (a) 5   (b) 5   (c) 4   (d) 3

2. (a) 23   (b) 6   (c) 22

Challenge: Teacher check

SHARING

1. Complete the pictures and write the answer. The first has been done for you.

e.g.   Share 12 marbles into 3 marble bags.

How many in each bag?

 = ___4___

(a)   Share 15 flowers among 3 vases.

How many in each vase? _____

(b)   Share 20 birds into 4 bird baths.

How many in each bird bath? _____

(c)   Share 8 eggs between 2 baskets.

How many in each basket? _____

(d)   Share 9 biscuits among 3 jars.

How many in each jar? _____

2. Share the place value blocks into equal groups.

(a)

(b)

(c)

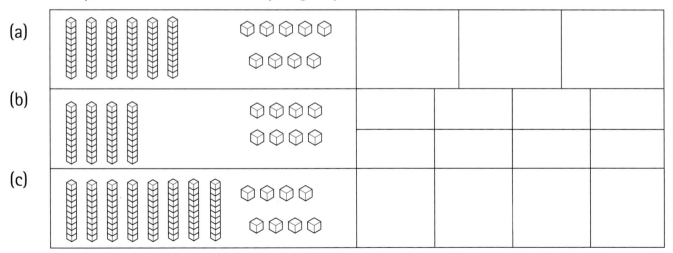

CHALLENGE   Write your own sharing problem to match this: 24 shared among 8.

_____

_____ = _____

Objective   *Understands division as sharing.*

TEACHER INFORMATION

MULTIPLICATION AND DIVISION

Objective

- Recall and use division facts for the 3, 4 and 8 multiplication tables.

Oral work and mental calculation

- Use the vocabulary: *divide*, *share* and *halve*.

- Complete practical sharing and grouping tasks, verbalising actions; for example,

  Sharing: 6 apples are shared between 3 horses. How many apples does each horse get?

  Grouping: There are 20 sweets in a jar. How many bags of 4 sweets can be made?

- Solve division calculations by using multiplication strategies; for example,

  Calculate 15 ÷ 3 by counting how many jumps of 3 are needed on a number line to reach 15.

- Respond rapidly to oral questions phrased in a variety of ways; for example,

  Share 15 between 3, How many eights make 64?, Divide 24 by 4, Is 21 a multiple of 3?

Main teaching activity

Division (page 85)

Additional activities suitable for developing the objective

- Solve division word problems; for example,

  A baker bakes 24 buns. 3 buns are put into each box. How many boxes will the baker need?

  Ainsley has used 12 tiles to make a pattern. One tile in every four is red. How many tiles are red?

- Use counters or a number line to work out the unknown numbers; for example,

  16 ÷ 4 = ___, 24 ÷ ___ = 3, ___ ÷ 3 = 8

Answers

1. (a) 4   (b) 8   (c) 6   (d) 2
   (e) 10   (f) 3   (g) 7   (h) 5
   (i) 9   (j) 3   (k) 5   (l) 7
   (m) 4   (n) 8   (o) 10   (p) 6
   (q) 8   (r) 5   (s) 2   (t) 6
   (u) 9   (v) 3   (w) 7   (x) 4

2. (b) 24 ÷ 8 = 3, 24 ÷ 3 = 8
   (c) 36 ÷ 9 = 4, 36 ÷ 4 = 9
   (d) 20 ÷ 4 = 5, 20 ÷ 5 = 4
   (e) 64 ÷ 8 = 8, 64 ÷ 8 = 8
   (f) 72 ÷ 8 = 9, 72 ÷ 9 = 8

3. 24 ÷ 3 = 8 and 8 x 3 = 24,
   40 ÷ 4 = 10 and 10 x 4 = 40,
   48 ÷ 6 = 8 and 8 x 6 = 48,
   32 ÷ 4 = 8 and 8 x 4 = 32,
   27 ÷ 3 = 9 and 3 x 9 = 27,
   80 ÷ 8 = 10 and 8 x 10 = 80

Challenge: 8 boxes

1. Complete these division facts.

(a) 12 ÷ 3 = _____   (b) 24 ÷ 3 = _____   (c) 18 ÷ 3 = _____   (d) 6 ÷ 3 = _____

(e) 30 ÷ 3 = _____   (f) 9 ÷ 3 = _____   (g) 21 ÷ 3 = _____   (h) 15 ÷ 3 = _____

(i) 36 ÷ 4 = _____   (j) 12 ÷ 4 = _____   (k) 20 ÷ 4 = _____   (l) 28 ÷ 4 = _____

(m) 16 ÷ 4 = _____   (n) 32 ÷ 4 = _____   (o) 40 ÷ 4 = _____   (p) 24 ÷ 4 = _____

(q) 80 ÷ 10 = _____   (r) 50 ÷ 10 = _____   (s) 20 ÷ 10 = _____   (t) 60 ÷ 10 = _____

(u) 90 ÷ 10 = _____   (v) 30 ÷ 10 = _____   (w) 70 ÷ 10 = _____   (x) 40 ÷ 10 = _____

2. Write two division facts using each set of numbers.

(a) | 3, 6, 18 | = | 18 | ÷ | 6 | = | 3 | and | 18 | ÷ | 3 | = | 6 |

(b) | 3, 8, 24 | = | ☐ | ÷ | ☐ | = | ☐ | and | ☐ | ÷ | ☐ | = | ☐ |

(c) | 4, 9, 36 | = | ☐ | ÷ | ☐ | = | ☐ | and | ☐ | ÷ | ☐ | = | ☐ |

(d) | 4, 5, 20 | = | ☐ | ÷ | ☐ | = | ☐ | and | ☐ | ÷ | ☐ | = | ☐ |

(e) | 8, 8, 64 | = | ☐ | ÷ | ☐ | = | ☐ | and | ☐ | ÷ | ☐ | = | ☐ |

(f) | 8, 9, 72 | = | ☐ | ÷ | ☐ | = | ☐ | and | ☐ | ÷ | ☐ | = | ☐ |

3. Draw lines to match each division fact to the corresponding multiplication fact.

| 32 ÷ 4 = 8 | 24 ÷ 3 = 8 | 40 ÷ 4 = 10 | 27 ÷ 3 = 9 | 48 ÷ 6 = 8 | 80 ÷ 8 = 10 |

| 10 x 4 = 40 | 8 x 10 = 80 | 8 x 4 = 32 | 8 x 6 = 48 | 8 x 3 = 24 | 3 x 9 = 27 |

CHALLENGE

A baker has baked 32 buns. 4 buns are put into each box.
How many boxes will the baker need?

Objective   *Derives and recalls ÷ 3, ÷ 4 and ÷ 8 facts.*

TEACHER INFORMATION

MULTIPLICATION AND DIVISION

Objective

- Recall and use division facts for the 3, 4 and 8 multiplication tables.

Oral work and mental calculation

- Use the vocabulary *remainder* and *left over*.

- Practise sharing using concrete materials; for example, share 17 beads into 3 boxes. How many beads are in each box? How many beads are left over?

- Give a whole number remainder when one number is divided by another; for example,

  Work out that 16 ÷ 3 = 5 r 1 and
  17 ÷ 4 = 4 r 1.

- Respond to oral questions such as finding how many are left over or how much is left when you:

  Share 18 between 4.

  Divide 45 by 8.

  Cut as many 8 cm lengths of ribbon as you can from 73 cm of ribbon.

Interactive whiteboard activity

Interactive whiteboard activity available to support this copymaster. Visit *www.prim-ed.com*.

Main teaching activity

Division with remainders (page 87)

Additional activities suitable for developing the objective

- Complete the unknown number to find remainders; for example,

  85 = 10 x 8 + ___ and 28 = 9 x 3 + ___.

- Solve word problems involving division with remainders. Use examples relevant to the pupils as you go about the day at school; for example,

  If there are 25 pupils in the class and you have 52 cakes to share at break, how many cakes will each pupil have and how many will be left over?

  If there are 25 pupils and 10 coat pegs how many pupils will not be able to hang up their coats if we put two coats on each peg?

Answers

1. 2, 1

2. (a) 4, 1   (b) 3, 2   (c) 3, 1   (d) 4, 2

Challenge: Teacher check (a) 4 (b) 2

DIVISION WITH REMAINDERS

1. Share seven eggs between three nests. Complete the number sentence.

7 eggs shared between 3 nests equals _____ eggs in each nest and _____ egg left over.

2. Draw the pictures and complete the number sentences.

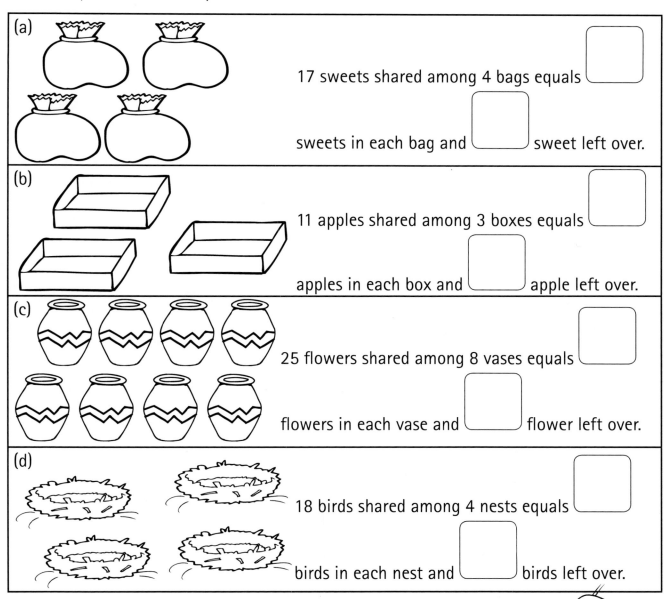

(a) 17 sweets shared among 4 bags equals ☐

sweets in each bag and ☐ sweet left over.

(b) 11 apples shared among 3 boxes equals ☐

apples in each box and ☐ apple left over.

(c) 25 flowers shared among 8 vases equals ☐

flowers in each vase and ☐ flower left over.

(d) 18 birds shared among 4 nests equals ☐

birds in each nest and ☐ birds left over.

CHALLENGE On the back of this sheet, draw this problem:
34 marbles shared between 8 children.

(a) How many marbles will each child have? _____

(b) How many marbles will be left over? _____

Objective   *Solves division problems by sharing objects using diagrams.*

TEACHER INFORMATION

MULTIPLICATION AND DIVISION

Objectives

- Recall and use division facts for the 3, 4 and 8 multiplication tables.
- Solve problems involving division.

Oral work and mental calculation

- Use the vocabulary *remainder* and *left over*.

- Practise sharing using concrete materials; for example, share 17 beads into 3 boxes. How many beads are in each box? How many beads are left over?

- Give a whole number remainder when one number is divided by another; for example,

  Work out that $16 \div 3 = 5$ r 1 and $17 \div 4 = 4$ r 1.

- Respond to oral questions such as finding how many are left over or how much is left when you:

  Share 18 between 4.

  Divide 45 by 8.

  Cut as many 8 cm lengths of ribbon as you can from 73 cm of ribbon.

Main teaching activity

Division (page 89)

Additional activities suitable for developing the objectives

- Complete the unknown number to find remainders; for example,

  $85 = 10 \times 8 +$ ___ and $28 = 9 \times 3 +$ ___.

- Solve word problems involving division with remainders. Use examples relevant to the pupils as you go about the day at school; for example,

  If there are 25 pupils in the class and you have 52 cakes to share at break, how many cakes will each pupil have and how many will be left over?

  If there are 25 pupils and 10 coat pegs how many pupils will not be able to hang up their coats if we put two coats on each peg?

Answers

1. share, divided by, shared between

2. (a) $20 \div 4 = 5$ (b) $12 \div 3 = 4$
   (c) $16 \div 4 = 4$ (d) $21 \div 3 = 7$
   (e) $16 \div 2 = 8$

3. (a) 5   (b) 5   (c) 3   (d) 5
   (e) 6   (f) 6   (g) 8   (h) 7
   (i) 4   (j) 5 r 1   (k) 5 r 3   (l) 4 r 2
   (m) 3 r 3   (n) 4 r 7   (o) 6 r 2

Challenge: Teacher check

DIVISION

1. Circle the words that mean the same as the symbol ÷.

   share   groups of   add   divided by   subtract   shared between

2. Use counters to help you write and solve these division problems.
   The first one is done for you.

e.g. 15 divided by 3		$15 \div 3 = \underline{\ \ 5\ \ }$
(a) 20 divided by 4		_____ ÷ _____ = _____
(b) 12 divided by 3		_____ ÷ _____ = _____
(c) 16 divided by 4		_____ ÷ _____ = _____
(d) 21 divided by 3		_____ ÷ _____ = _____
(e) 16 divided by 2		_____ ÷ _____ = _____

3. Use counters to help solve these division problems.

   (a) $40 \div 8 =$ _____   (b) $15 \div 3 =$ _____   (c) $15 \div 5 =$ _____

   (d) $20 \div 4 =$ _____   (e) $18 \div 3 =$ _____   (f) $24 \div 4 =$ _____

   (g) $16 \div 2 =$ _____   (h) $21 \div 3 =$ _____   (i) $28 \div 8 =$ _____

   (j) $16 \div 3 =$ _____ remainder _____   (k) $23 \div 4 =$ _____ remainder _____

   (l) $18 \div 4 =$ _____ remainder _____   (m) $27 \div 8 =$ _____ remainder _____

   (n) $39 \div 8 =$ _____ remainder _____   (o) $20 \div 3 =$ _____ remainder _____

CHALLENGE   Check your answers. Tick (✔) them if they are correct and cross (✗) them if they are incorrect. Redo the incorrect sums on the back of the sheet.

Objective   *Uses written methods and sharing concepts to solve division problems with and without remainders.*

TEACHER INFORMATION

MULTIPLICATION AND DIVISION

Objectives

- Recall and use division facts for the 3, 4 and 8 multiplication tables.

- Solve problems involving division.

Oral work and mental calculation

- Use the vocabulary *remainder* and *left over*.

- Practise sharing using concrete materials; for example, share 17 beads into 3 boxes. How many beads are in each box? How many beads are left over?

- Give a whole number remainder when one number is divided by another; for example,

  Work out that 16 ÷ 3 = 5 r 1 and 17 ÷ 4 = 4 r 1.

- Respond to oral questions such as finding how many are left over or how much is left when you:

  Share 18 between 4.

  Divide 45 by 8.

  Cut as many 8 cm lengths of ribbon as you can from 73 cm of ribbon.

Interactive whiteboard activity

Interactive whiteboard activity available to support this copymaster. Visit *www.prim-ed.com*.

Main teaching activity

Dividing (page 91)

Additional activities suitable for developing the objectives

- Complete the unknown number to find remainders; for example,

  85 = 10 x 8 + ___ and 28 = 9 x 3 + ___.

- Solve word problems involving division with remainders. Use examples relevant to the pupils as you go about the day at school; for example,

  If there are 25 pupils in the class and you have 52 cakes to share at break, how many cakes will each pupil have and how many will be left over?

  If there are 25 pupils and 10 coat pegs how many pupils will not be able to hang up their coats if we put two coats on each peg?

Answers

1. (a) 15 ÷ 3 = 5 (b) 18 ÷ 3 = 6
   (c) 24 ÷ 8 = 3 (d) 16 ÷ 4 = 4
   (e) 20 ÷ 4 = 5

2. (a) 4   (b) 8   (c) 4   (d) 9
   (e) 3 r 2 (f) 4 r 2 (g) 4 r 1 (h) 2 r 6

Challenge: 23 ÷ 4 = 5 r 3

Another word for sharing is dividing or division. We also use the sign ÷ to represent this process. If a number cannot be equally shared there may be a remainder.

1. Write the division problem and solve it. The first one has been done for you.

e.g. Share 20 oranges among 4 bowls. How many in each bowl? __20__ ÷ __4__ = __5__	(a) Share 15 people among 3 cars. How many in each car? _____ ÷ _____ = _____
(b) Share 18 dogs among 3 kennels. How many in each kennel? _____ ÷ _____ = _____	(c) Share 24 birds among 8 trees. How many in each tree? _____ ÷ _____ = _____
(d) Share 16 jelly beans among 4 children. How many jelly beans each? _____ ÷ _____ = _____	(e) Share 20 flowers among 4 bushes. How many on each bush? _____ ÷ _____ = _____

2. Use counters to solve these division problems. If a number cannot be equally shared there may be a remainder.

(a) 16 counters divided into 4 groups = _____

(b) 24 counters divided into 3 groups = _____

(c) 32 counters divided into 8 groups = _____

(d) 36 counters divided into 4 groups = _____

(e) 11 counters divided into 3 groups = _____ remainder _____

(f) 14 counters divided into 3 groups = _____ remainder _____

(g) 17 counters divided into 4 groups = _____ remainder _____

(h) 22 counters divided into 8 groups = _____ remainder _____

CHALLENGE Share 23 sweets among 4 people. How many sweets does each person get?

Number sentence: _____ ÷ _____ = _____ remainder _____

Objective *Uses written methods and sharing concepts to solve division problems with and without remainders.*

MULTIPLICATION AND DIVISION

Objective

- Recall and use division facts for the 3, 4 and 8 multiplication tables.

Oral work and mental calculation

- Use the vocabulary: *divide*, *share* and *halve*.

- Answer oral questions; for example,

  You know that 6 x 3 = 18. So what is: 18 ÷ 3? 18 ÷ 6?

  You know that 12 ÷ 4 = 3. So what is 3 x 4? 4 x 3?

- Give three numbers such as 3, 8 and 24. Say two different multiplication and two different division statements using those numbers.

- Solve division calculations by using multiplication strategies; for example,

  Calculate 15 ÷ 3 by counting how many jumps of 3 are needed on a number line to reach 15.

  Solve 18 ÷ 3 by interpreting this as 'How many threes make 18?'

Interactive whiteboard activity

Interactive whiteboard activity available to support this copymaster. Visit *www.prim-ed.com*.

Main teaching activity

Multiplication and division (page 93)

Additional activities suitable for developing the objective

- Give out cards; for example, 10 x 3 = 30, 30 ÷ 10 = 3, 2 x 4 = 8, 8 ÷ 2 = 4. Match the cards. Play 'Snap'.

- Write two multiplication and two division sentences, using a set of three given numbers; for example, 3, 8 and 24.

- Complete sums with symbols standing for unknown numbers; for example, 15 ÷ 3 = ☐, 3 x 5 = ☐, 5 x 3 = ☐

- Use multiplication to check division and vice versa, as a strategy when checking work.

Answers

1. (a) 4
   (b) 4
   (c) 40, 40 ÷ 5 = 8 / 40 ÷ 8 = 5
   (d) 30, 30 ÷ 10 = 3 / 30 ÷ 3 = 10
   (e) 24, 24 ÷ 4 = 6 / 24 ÷ 6 = 4
   (f) 32, 32 ÷ 4 = 8 / 32 ÷ 8 = 4
   (g) 27, 27 ÷ 3 = 9 / 27 ÷ 9 = 3
   (h) 40, 40 ÷ 10 = 4 / 40 ÷ 4 = 10
   (i) 20, 20 ÷ 5 = 4 / 20 ÷ 4 = 5
   (j) 8, 8 ÷ 1 = 8 / 8 ÷ 8 = 1

2. (a) 4 x 8 = 32 (b) 7 x 4 = 28
   (c) 8 x 10 = 80 (d) 8 x 3 = 24
   (e) 4 x 4 = 16 (f) 7 x 3 = 21

Challenge: Teacher check

MULTIPLICATION AND DIVISION

1. Fill in the related division facts from these multiplication facts;
   e.g. 7 x 3 = 21   21 ÷ 3 = 7

(a) 4 x 2 = ___8___   8 ÷ 2 = _____

(b) 4 x 3 = ___12___   12 ÷ 3 = _____

(c) 8 x 5 = _____   _____ ÷ _____ = _____

(d) 3 x 10 = _____   _____ ÷ _____ = _____

(e) 6 x 4 = _____   _____ ÷ _____ = _____

(f) 4 x 8 = _____   _____ ÷ _____ = _____

(g) 9 x 3 = _____   _____ ÷ _____ = _____

(h) 4 x 10 = _____   _____ ÷ _____ = _____

(i) 5 x 4 = _____   _____ ÷ _____ = _____

(j) 8 x 1 = _____   _____ ÷ _____ = _____

2. Draw lines to match the division fact with its matching multiplication fact.

(a) 32 ÷ 8 = 4   •   • 8 x 10 = 80

(b) 28 ÷ 4 = 7   •   • 4 x 4 = 16

(c) 80 ÷ 8 = 10   •   • 7 x 3 = 21

(d) 24 ÷ 3 = 8   •   • 4 x 8 = 32

(e) 16 ÷ 4 = 4   •   • 8 x 3 = 24

(f) 21 ÷ 3 = 7   •   • 7 x 4 = 28

CHALLENGE

On the back of this sheet, write out the 4 times table and matching division facts;
e.g. 1 x 4 = 4 and 4 ÷ 4 = 1, 2 x 4 = 8 and 8 ÷ 4 = 2.

Objective   *Uses known multiplication facts to solve division problems.*

TEACHER INFORMATION

MULTIPLICATION AND DIVISION

Objective

- Write and calculate mathematical statements for multiplication using the multiplication tables that they know, using mental methods.

Oral work and mental calculation

- Demonstrate and discuss the effect of multiplying by 10. Extend to multiplying by 100.

- Respond quickly to questions; for example,
  53 x 10   79 x 10   84 x 100   27 x 100

- Give pupils a number and an answer; for example, 35 and 350. Ask pupils whether the number has been multiplied by 10 or 100.

Interactive whiteboard activity

Interactive whiteboard activity available to support this copymaster. Visit *www.prim-ed.com*.

Main teaching activity

Multiplying by 10 or 100 (page 95)

Additional activities suitable for developing the objective

- Complete the missing numbers in x10/x100 sums; for example,

  7 x 10 = ☐   5 x ☐ = 500

- Solve word problems involving x10 and x100; for example, How many toes on five pairs of feet? Twelve jars each contain 100 sweets. How many sweets altogether?

Answers

1. (a) 20, 200, 30, 300, 40, 400, 50, 500, 60, 600, 70, 700, 80, 800, 90, 900, 100, 1000
   (b) and (c) Teacher check

2. (a) 27, 270, 2700   (b) 54, 540, 5400
   (c) 89, 890, 8900

3. (a) 39, 39, 390, 3900   (b) 41, 41, 410, 4100
   (c) 58, 58, 580, 5800   (d) 72, 72, 720, 7200
   (e) 80, 80, 800, 8000   (f) 96, 96, 960, 9600

Challenge: (a) 630   (b) 6300   (c) 63 000

MULTIPLYING BY 10 OR 100

1. (a) Complete the x10 and x100 table.

Number	1	2	3	4	5	6	7	8	9	10
x 10	10									
x 100	100									

(b) Describe what happens when numbers are multiplied by 10.

_____

_____

(c) Describe what happens when numbers are multiplied by 100.

_____

_____

2. Complete the multiplication sums.

(a) 27 x 1   = _____   (b) 54 x 1   = _____   (c) 89 x 1   = _____

   27 x 10   = _____   54 x 10   = _____   89 x 10   = _____

   27 x 100 = _____   54 x 100 = _____   89 x 100 = _____

3. Draw lines to match each number.

number	x1	x10	x100
24	39	240	7200
(a) 39	58	410	5800
(b) 41	80	580	9600
(c) 58	24	390	8000
(d) 72	96	720	2400
(e) 80	41	800	4100
(f) 96	72	960	3900

CHALLENGE Complete the multiplication sums.

(a) 63 x 10 = _____   (b) 63 x 100 = _____   (c) 63 x 1000 = _____

Objective   *Multiplies one- and two-digit numbers by 10 and 100.*

TEACHER INFORMATION

MULTIPLICATION AND DIVISION

Objective

- Write and calculate mathematical statements for multiplication using the multiplication tables that they know, including for two-digit numbers times one-digit numbers, using formal written methods.

Oral work and mental calculation

- Chant the 2/3/4/5/8/10 times tables – forwards and backwards.

- Respond quickly to oral questions phrased in a variety of ways; for example, Six twos, 3 times 4, 5 multiplied by 3, Multiply 4 by 5, How many tens in 80?, Divide 24 by 4.

- Play 'Tables knockout'. All pupils stand in a circle. Pair up pupils and ask them a question from the 2/3/4/5/8/10 times table. The pupil who answers correctly remains standing. The other pupil sits down. The winner is the last pupil left standing.

- Practise partitioning two-digit numbers into tens and ones; for example, 23 = 20 + 3.

- Practise adding multiples of 10 (such as 20 and 30) using the related addition fact 2 + 3.

- Demonstrate and discuss how to multiply using partitioning.

Main teaching activity

Multiplication using partitioning (page 97)

Additional activities suitable for developing the objective

- Play 'Tables dominoes' and 'Tables bingo'.

- Play 'Maths snap', using cards made with 2/3/4/5/8/10 multiplication facts and the related division facts.

- Partition two-digit numbers in writing; for example, 48 = 40 + 8.

- Practise multiplication sums in writing, using the partitioning method.

Answers

1. Teacher check

2. (a) 54   (b) 85   (c) 96   (d) 232
   (e) 70   (f) 205   (g) 224

Challenge: 252 books

MULTIPLICATION USING PARTITIONING

1. Complete the multiplication table.

x	7	2	6	8	1	5	9	3	10	4
2										
3										
4										
5										
8										
10										

2. Use partitioning to solve these multiplication sums.

Example: 15 x 4

15 x 4 = (10 + 5) x 4
= (10 x 4) + (5 x 4)
= 40 + 20 = 60

(a) 18 x 3 = (___ + __8__) x ___

= (__10__ x ___) + (___ x __3__)

= ___ + ___ = ___

(b) 17 x 5 = (___ + ___) x ___

= (___ x ___) + (___ x ___)

= ___ + ___ = ___

(c) 24 x 4 = (___ + ___) x ___

= (___ x ___) + (___ x ___)

= ___ + ___ = ___

(d) 29 x 8 = (___ + ___) x ___

= (___ x ___) + (___ x ___)

= ___ + ___ = ___

(e) 35 x 2 = (___ + ___) x ___

= (___ x ___) + (___ x ___)

= ___ + ___ = ___

(f) 41 x 5 = (___ + ___) x ___

= (___ x ___) + (___ x ___)

= ___ + ___ = ___

(g) 56 x 4 = (___ + ___) x ___

= (___ x ___) + (___ x ___)

= ___ + ___ = ___

CHALLENGE On the back of this sheet, use partitioning to solve this problem.
There are 4 bookshelves. Each bookshelf holds 63 books. How many books are there altogether?

Objective *Solves multiplication sums using partitioning.*

TEACHER INFORMATION

MULTIPLICATION AND DIVISION

Objective

- Write and calculate mathematical statements for multiplication using the multiplication tables that they know, including for two-digit numbers times one-digit numbers, using formal written methods.

Oral work and mental calculation

- Chant the 2/3/4/5/8/10 times tables – forwards and backwards.

- Respond quickly to oral questions phrased in a variety of ways; for example, Six twos, 3 times 4, 5 multiplied by 3, Multiply 4 by 5, How many tens in 80?, Divide 24 by 4.

- Play 'Tables knockout'. All pupils stand in a circle. Pair up pupils and ask them a question from the 2/3/4/5/8/10 times table. The pupil who answers correctly remains standing. The other pupil sits down. The winner is the last pupil left standing.

- Practise partitioning two-digit numbers into tens and ones; for example, 23 = 20 + 3.

- Practise adding multiples of 10 (such as 20 and 30) using the related addition fact 2 + 3.

- Demonstrate and discuss how to multiply using the grid method.

Interactive whiteboard activity

Interactive whiteboard activity available to support this copymaster. Visit *www.prim-ed.com*.

Main teaching activity

Multiplication using the grid method (page 99)

Additional activities suitable for developing the objective

- Play 'Tables dominoes' and 'Tables bingo'.

- Play 'Maths snap', using cards made with 2/3/4/5/8/10 multiplication facts and the related division facts.

- Partition two-digit numbers in writing; for example, 48 = 40 + 8.

- Practise multiplication sums in writing, using the grid method.

- Answer TU x U word problems using an appropriate written method.

Answers

1. (a) 135   (b) 72   (c) 117   (d) 336
   (e) 96   (f) 204   (g) 189   (h) 272
   (i) 395   (j) 672

2. (a) 78 marbles   (b) 190 nuts

Challenge: 600 passengers

MULTIPLICATION USING THE GRID METHOD

1. Use the grid method to solve these multiplication sums.

Example: 35 x 4

x	4
30	120
5	20
	140

(30 x 4 = 120)

(5 x 4 = 20)

(120 + 20 = 140)

(a) 27 x 5

x	

(b) 36 x 2

x	

(c) 39 x 3

x	

(d) 42 x 8

x	

(e) 48 x 2

x	

(f) 51 x 4

x	

(g) 63 x 3

x	

(h) 68 x 4

x	

(i) 79 x 5

x	

(j) 84 x 8

x	

2. Solve these multiplication problems.

(a) 3 children each have 26 marbles. How many marbles altogether?

x	

(b) 5 packets of nuts each contain 38 nuts. How many nuts altogether?

x	

CHALLENGE On the back of the sheet, use the grid method to solve this problem.

There are 8 aeroplanes. Each aeroplane carries 75 passengers. How many passengers altogether?

Objective *Solves multiplication using the grid method.*

TEACHER INFORMATION

MULTIPLICATION AND DIVISION

Objective

- Write and calculate mathematical statements for multiplication using the multiplication tables that they know, including for two-digit numbers times one-digit numbers, using formal written methods.

Oral work and mental calculation

- Chant the 2/3/4/5/8/10 times tables – forwards and backwards.

- Respond quickly to oral questions phrased in a variety of ways; for example, Six twos, 3 times 4, 5 multiplied by 3, Multiply 4 by 5, How many tens in 80?, Divide 24 by 4.

- Play 'Tables knockout'. All pupils stand in a circle. Pair up pupils and ask them a question from the 2/3/4/5/8/10 times table. The pupil who answers correctly remains standing. The other pupil sits down. The winner is the last pupil left standing.

- Practise partitioning two-digit numbers into tens and ones; for example, 23 = 20 + 3.

- Practise adding multiples of 10 (such as 20 and 30) using the related addition fact 2 + 3.

- Demonstrate and discuss how to multiply using the expanded short multiplication and short multiplication methods.

Main teaching activity

Short multiplication (page 101)

Additional activities suitable for developing the objective

- Play 'Tables dominoes' and 'Tables bingo'.

- Play 'Maths snap', using cards made with 2/3/4/5/8/10 multiplication facts and the related division facts.

- Partition two-digit numbers in writing; for example, 48 = 40 + 8.

- Practise multiplication sums in writing, using the short multiplication method.

- Answer TU x U word problems using the appropriate written method.

Answers

1.	(a) 92	(b) 78	(c) 210	(d) 424
	(e) 207	(f) 576		

2.	(a) 28	(b) 50	(c) 105	(d) 240
	(e) 68	(f) 164	(g) 57	(h) 168
	(i) 168	(j) 99		

Challenge: 66 oranges

SHORT MULTIPLICATION

1. Use the expanded short multiplication method to solve these sums.

Example: 25 x 3

```
   25
x   3
─────
   15    (5 x 3 = 15)
   60    (20 x 3 = 60)
─────
   75    (15 + 60 = 75)
```

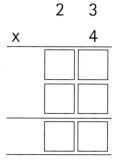

(a)
```
     2 3
x      4
```

(b)
```
     3 9
x      2
```

(c)
```
     4 2
x      5
```

(d)
```
     5 3
x      8
```

(e)
```
     6 9
x      3
```

(f)
```
     7 2
x      8
```

2. Complete these 2-digit by 1-digit short multiplication problems. Remember to start in the ones column.

Example:
```
     2 3
x      2
─────
  ④ 6
```
3 x 2 = 6
20 x 2 = 40

(a)
```
     1 4
x      2
─────
```

(b)
```
     1 0
x      5
─────
```

(c)
```
     2 1
x      5
─────
```

(d)
```
     3 0
x      8
─────
```

(e)
```
     3 4
x      2
─────
```

(f)
```
     4 1
x      4
─────
```

(g)
```
     5 7
x      1
─────
```

(h)
```
     4 2
x      4
─────
```

(i)
```
     2 1
x      8
─────
```

(j)
```
     3 3
x      3
─────
```

CHALLENGE

Write the number sentence to solve the problem.

At the fruit shop there are three boxes of oranges. If each box holds 22, how many oranges are there altogether?

TEACHER INFORMATION

MULTIPLICATION AND DIVISION

Objective

- Write and calculate mathematical statements for multiplication using the multiplication tables that they know, using formal written methods.

Oral work and mental calculation

- Use the vocabulary: *remainder* and *left over*.

- Give a whole number remainder when one number is divided by another; for example,

  Work out that $16 \div 3 = 5$ r 1 and $75 \div 10 = 7$ r 5.

- Respond to oral questions such as finding how many are left over or how much is left when you:

  Share 16 between 5.

  Divide 45 by 10.

  Cut as many 10 cm lengths of ribbon as you can from 73 cm of ribbon.

- Practise partitioning two-digit numbers into tens and ones; for example, $49 = 40 + 9$

- Demonstrate and discuss how to divide using partitioning.

Main teaching activity

Division using partitioning (page 103)

Additional activities suitable for developing the objective

- Complete the unknown number to find remainders; for example,

  $54 = 10 \times 5 + \boxed{}$ and $27 = 5 \times 5 + \boxed{}$.

- Solve word problems involving division with remainders. Use examples relevant to the pupils as you go about the day at school; for example,

  If there are 25 pupils in the class and you have 52 cakes to share at break, how many cakes will each pupil have and how many will be left over?

  If there are 25 pupils and 10 coat pegs how many pupils will not be able to hang up their coats if we put two coats on each peg?

- Partition two-digit numbers in writing; for example, $85 = 80 + 5$.

- Practise division sums in writing, using the partitioning method.

- Answer TU ÷ U word problems using an appropriate written method.

Answers

1. (a) 15   (b) 14   (c) 13   (d) 12   (e) 19

2. (a) 13   (b) 23   (c) 13

Challenge: Teacher check

DIVISION USING PARTITIONING

1. Use partitioning to solve these division sums.

Example: 32 ÷ 2
32 ÷ 2 = (20 + 12) ÷ 2
= (20 ÷ 2) + (12 ÷ 2)
= 10 + 6 = 16

(a) 45 ÷ 3 = (__30__ + ____) ÷ ____

= (____ ÷ __3__) + (__15__ ÷ ____)

= ____ + ____ = ____

(b) 56 ÷ 4 = (____ + ____) ÷ ____

= (____ ÷ ____) + (____ ÷ ____)

= ____ + ____ = ____

(c) 65 ÷ 5 = (____ + ____) ÷ ____

= (____ ÷ ____) + (____ ÷ ____)

= ____ + ____ = ____

(d) 96 ÷ 8 = (____ + ____) ÷ ____

= (____ ÷ ____) + (____ ÷ ____)

= ____ + ____ = ____

(e) 38 ÷ 2 = (____ + ____) ÷ ____

= (____ ÷ ____) + (____ ÷ ____)

= ____ + ____ = ____

2. Use partitioning to solve these word problems.

(a) 39 pencils shared among 3 children. How many pencils each?

____ ÷ ____ = (____ + ____) ÷ ____

= (____ ÷ ____) + (____ ÷ ____)

= ____ + ____ = ____

(b) 46 sweets shared among 2 children. How many sweets each?

____ ÷ ____ = (____ + ____) ÷ ____

= (____ ÷ ____) + (____ ÷ ____)

= ____ + ____ = ____

(c) 52 biscuits shared among 4 people. How many biscuits each?

____ ÷ ____ = (____ + ____) ÷ ____

= (____ ÷ ____) + (____ ÷ ____)

= ____ + ____ = ____

CHALLENGE

Check your answers. Tick (✔) them if they are correct and cross (✗) them if they are incorrect. Redo the incorrect sums on the back of the sheet.

Objective   *Solves division sums using partitioning.*

TEACHER INFORMATION

MULTIPLICATION AND DIVISION

Objective

- Write and calculate mathematical statements for multiplication using the multiplication tables that they know, using formal written methods.

Oral work and mental calculation

- Estimate answers to division sums using rounding, before completing them, as a checking strategy.

- Experiment with different pencil and paper methods of working out division problems. Explain orally how methods work.

- Demonstrate TU ÷ U sums, first without and then with remainders.

- Explain that when calculations are set out in columns, tens should be under tens and units under units.

Interactive whiteboard activity

Interactive whiteboard activity available to support this copymaster. Visit *www.prim-ed.com*.

Main teaching activity

Short division (page 105)

Additional activities suitable for developing the objective

- Estimate answers to division sums using rounding, before completing them, as a checking strategy.

- Complete a 10 x 10 multiplication grid.

- Complete TU ÷ U sums, first without and then with remainders.

- Solve word problems involving TU ÷ U.

Answers

1.	(a) 5	(b) 2	(c) 6	(d) 3	(e) 13

2.	(a) 7	(b) 4	(c) 9	(d) 9
	(e) 5	(f) 11	(g) 9	(h) 8
	(i) 14	(j) 7	(k) 12	(l) 12

3.	(a) 24	(b) 32	(c) 12	(d) 9

Challenge: Teacher check

SHORT DIVISION

1. Use the counters to help you write and solve these division sums. The first one is done for you.

16 divided by 4	⟨counters⟩	$4\overline{)16}$ with 4 above
(a) 15 divided by 3	⟨counters⟩	$3\overline{)15}$
(b) 16 divided by 8	⟨counters⟩	$8\overline{)16}$
(c) 24 divided by 4	⟨counters⟩	$4\overline{)24}$
(d) 21 divided by 7	⟨counters⟩	$7\overline{)21}$
(e) 26 divided by 2	⟨counters⟩	$2\overline{)26}$

2. Solve these division problems.

(a) $2\overline{)14}$ (b) $8\overline{)32}$ (c) $3\overline{)27}$ (d) $4\overline{)36}$

(e) $8\overline{)40}$ (f) $10\overline{)110}$ (g) $5\overline{)45}$ (h) $8\overline{)64}$

(i) $10\overline{)140}$ (j) $4\overline{)28}$ (k) $5\overline{)60}$ (l) $3\overline{)36}$

3. (a) Divide forty-eight by two.

(b) Divide ninety-six by three.

(c) Divide three into thirty-six.

(d) Divide eight into seventy-two.

CHALLENGE Check your answers. Tick them if they are correct and cross them if they are incorrect. Rework any incorrect solutions.

Objective   *Develops written methods for TU ÷ U.*

TEACHER INFORMATION

MULTIPLICATION AND DIVISION

Objective

- Solve problems, including missing number problems, involving multiplication and division.

Oral work and mental calculation

- Chant the 2/3/4/5/8/10 times tables – forwards and backwards.

- Respond quickly to oral questions phrased in a variety of ways; for example, Six twos, 3 times 10, 5 multiplied by 5, Multiply 4 by 5, How many tens in 80?, Divide 24 by 2.

- Play 'Tables knockout'. All pupils stand in a circle. Pair up pupils and ask them a question from the 2/3/4/5/8/10 times table. The pupil who answers correctly remains standing. The other pupil sits down. The winner is the last pupil left standing.

- Give pupils a multiplication fact and ask them to give a corresponding division fact and vice versa.

Interactive whiteboard activity

Interactive whiteboard activity available to support this copymaster. Visit *www.prim-ed.com*.

Main teaching activity

Multiplication and division inverses (page 107)

Additional activities suitable for developing the objective

- Play 'Tables dominoes' and 'Tables bingo'.

- Play 'Maths snap', using cards made with 2/3/4/5/8/10 multiplication facts and the related division facts.

- Give division facts (÷2/3/4/5/8/10) and time how long it takes for pupils to write the related multiplication facts.

Answers

1. 5 x 3 = 15 and 15 ÷ 3 = 5,
   9 x 4 = 36 and 36 ÷ 4 = 9,
   7 x 5 = 35 and 35 ÷ 5 = 7,
   2 x 8 = 16 and 16 ÷ 2 = 8,
   6 x 10 = 60 and 60 ÷ 6 = 10

2. 16 ÷ 4 = 4 and 4 x 4 = 16
   56 ÷ 8 = 7 and 8 x 7 = 56
   18 ÷ 2 = 9 and 9 x 2 = 18
   90 ÷ 10 = 9 and 10 x 9 = 90
   24 ÷ 3 = 8 and 3 x 8 = 24
   30 ÷ 5 = 6 and 5 x 6 = 30

3. (a) 30 and 30 ÷ 5 = 6 or 30 ÷ 6 = 5
   (b) 18 and 18 ÷ 2 = 9 or 18 ÷ 9 = 2
   (c) 32 and 32 ÷ 8 = 4 or 32 ÷ 4 = 8
   (d) 48 and 48 ÷ 8 = 6 or 48 ÷ 6 = 8
   (e) 4 and 4 x 10 = 40 or 10 x 4 = 40
   (f) 9 and 3 x 9 = 27 or 9 x 3 = 27
   (g) 9 and 9 x 5 = 45 or 5 x 9 = 45
   (h) 9 and 4 x 9 = 36 or 9 x 4 = 36

4. (a) 3 x 8 = 24, 8 x 3 = 24, 24 ÷ 3 = 8, 24 ÷ 8 = 3
   (b) 8 x 4 = 32, 4 x 8 = 32, 32 ÷ 8 = 4, 32 ÷ 4 = 8
   (c) 6 x 5 = 30, 5 x 6 = 30, 30 ÷ 6 = 5, 30 ÷ 5 = 6

Challenge: 15 x 5 = 75, 5 x 15 = 75,
75 ÷ 5 = 15, 75 ÷ 15 = 5

MULTIPLICATION AND DIVISION INVERSES

1. Match each multiplication fact to its matching division fact.

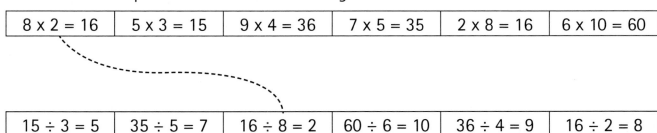

8 x 2 = 16	5 x 3 = 15	9 x 4 = 36	7 x 5 = 35	2 x 8 = 16	6 x 10 = 60

15 ÷ 3 = 5	35 ÷ 5 = 7	16 ÷ 8 = 2	60 ÷ 6 = 10	36 ÷ 4 = 9	16 ÷ 2 = 8

2. Match each division fact to its matching multiplication fact.

16 ÷ 4 = 4	56 ÷ 8 = 7	18 ÷ 2 = 9	90 ÷ 10 = 9	24 ÷ 3 = 8	30 ÷ 5 = 6

9 x 2 = 18	4 x 4 = 16	3 x 8 = 24	8 x 7 = 56	5 x 6 = 30	10 x 9 = 90

3. Complete the related facts.

(a) 6 x 5 = ____ and 30 ÷ ____ = ____

(b) 9 x 2 = ____ and ____ ÷ ____ = ____

(c) 8 x 4 = ____ and ____ ÷ ____ = ____

(d) 8 x 6 = ____ and ____ ÷ ____ = ____

(e) 40 ÷ 10 = ____ and __10__ x ____ = ____

(f) 27 ÷ 3 = ____ and ____ x ____ = ____

(g) 45 ÷ 5 = ____ and ____ x ____ = ____

(h) 36 ÷ 4 = ____ and ____ x ____ = ____

4. Write two multiplication and two division facts using each set of numbers.

(a) | 3, 8, 24 |

☐ x ☐ = ☐
☐ x ☐ = ☐
☐ ÷ ☐ = ☐
☐ ÷ ☐ = ☐

(b) | 32, 8, 4 |

☐ x ☐ = ☐
☐ x ☐ = ☐
☐ ÷ ☐ = ☐
☐ ÷ ☐ = ☐

(c) | 6, 30, 5 |

☐ x ☐ = ☐
☐ x ☐ = ☐
☐ ÷ ☐ = ☐
☐ ÷ ☐ = ☐

Write two multiplication and two division facts using the numbers 15, 75, 5.

☐ x ☐ = ☐ , ☐ x ☐ = ☐ , ☐ ÷ ☐ = ☐ , ☐ ÷ ☐ = ☐

Objective *Recognises that multiplication and division are inverse operations.*

TEACHER INFORMATION

MULTIPLICATION AND DIVISION

Objective

- Solve problems, including missing number problems, involving multiplication and division.

Oral work and mental calculation

- Respond rapidly to oral questions; for example,
  $3 \square 8 = 24$, $20 \square 10 = 2$.

- Work out the missing symbol in sums; for example,
  $3 \times 8 = ?$, $20 \div 10 = ?$

Interactive whiteboard activity

Interactive whiteboard activity available to support this copymaster. Visit *www.prim-ed.com*.

Main teaching activity

Unknown symbols and numbers (page 109)

Additional activities suitable for developing the objective

- Record sums using the symbols x, ÷ and =.

- Complete x and ÷ sums with a symbol representing a missing number or symbol; for example,

  $6 \times 2 = \square$ $25 \square 5 = 5$ $\square \times \triangle = 12$

- Make up number stories to reflect statements; for example, $15 \square 3 = 5$.

Answers

1. (a) x   (b) ÷   (c) ÷   (d) x
   (e) x   (f) ÷   (g) ÷   (h) x
   (i) ÷   (j) x   (k) x   (l) ÷

2. (a) 4   (b) 3   (c) 4   (d) 2
   (e) 10   (f) 8   (g) 5   (h) 2
   (i) 10   (j) 3   (k) 8   (l) 5

3. (a) 18   (b) x   (c) x   (d) 6
   (e) x   (f) x   (g) 8   (h) ÷
   (i) 8   (j) 8   (k) 72   (l) 8

Challenge: Teacher check

UNKNOWN SYMBOLS AND NUMBERS

1. Write the symbol x or ÷ into the box to complete each sum.

(a) 3 ☐ 4 = 12   (b) 15 ☐ 3 = 5   (c) 18 ☐ 2 = 9

(d) 5 ☐ 2 = 10   (e) 4 ☐ 4 = 16   (f) 20 ☐ 4 = 5

(g) 30 ☐ 5 = 6   (h) 8 ☐ 5 = 40   (i) 16 ☐ 8 = 2

(j) 8 ☐ 4 = 32   (k) 7 ☐ 10 = 70   (l) 50 ☐ 5 = 10

2. Write the missing number into the box to complete each multiplication sum.

(a) 5 x ☐ = 20   (b) 4 x ☐ = 12

(c) ☐ x 7 = 28   (d) 8 x ☐ = 16

(e) 5 x ☐ = 50   (f) 4 x ☐ = 32

(g) ☐ x 8 = 40   (h) 6 x ☐ = 12

(i) ☐ x 6 = 60   (j) ☐ x 9 = 27

(k) ☐ x 8 = 64   (l) 5 x ☐ = 25

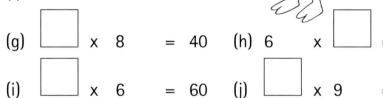

3. Write the missing number or symbol into the box to complete each multiplication and division sum.

(a) 9 x 2 = ☐   (b) 4 ☐ 10 = 40   (c) 5 ☐ 4 = 20

(d) 3 x ☐ = 18   (e) 7 ☐ 5 = 35   (f) 6 ☐ 8 = 48

(g) 40 ÷ 5 = ☐   (h) 36 ☐ 4 = 9   (i) 24 ÷ ☐ = 3

(j) 10 x ☐ = 80   (k) ☐ ÷ 8 = 9   (l) ☐ ÷ 2 = 4

CHALLENGE Write the missing numbers into each sum.

(a) ☐ x △ = 12   (b) ☐ ÷ △ = 4

△ x ☐ = 12   △ ÷ ☐ = 4

Objective *Recognises the use of a symbol to stand for an unknown number or operation.*

TEACHER INFORMATION

MULTIPLICATION AND DIVISION

Objective

- Solve problems involving multiplication, including positive integer scaling problems.

Oral work and mental calculation

- Orally answer one-step number problems; for example,

  Casey has 25 apples. Chloe has 4 times as many. How many apples does Chloe have?

- Encourage the pupils to explain how they worked out the answers.

- Play 'Think of a number'; for example,

  I am thinking of a number. It is three times more than 6. What is the number?

Interactive whiteboard activity

Interactive whiteboard activity available to support this copymaster. Visit *www.prim-ed.com*.

Main teaching activity

'Real life' word problems (page 111)

Additional activities suitable for developing the objective

- Complete word problems based on 'real life' experiences; for example,

  Dad drove 50 km and Mum drove 4 times as far. How far did Mum drive? How much further did Mum drive than Dad?

- Pupils write their own word problems about 'real life' and ask a partner to work them out.

Answers

1. (a) 125 daisies
   (b) 24 km
   (c) 15 storeys
   (d) 24 metres

2. Teacher check

Challenge: Teacher check

'REAL LIFE' WORD PROBLEMS

1. Solve the word problems showing calculations.

   (a) *There are 25 daisies in my garden, but my neighbour has five times as many. How many daisies are in my neighbour's garden?*

   (b) *Jess walked 4 km to the shops and Sophie walked six times as far. How far did Sophie walk?*

   (c) *Joseph lives in an apartment block with 5 storeys. Claire's apartment block is three times as high. How many storeys does Claire's apartment block have?*

   (d) *Class 4 made a line of pennies that was 8 metres in length. Class 3's line was three times as long. How long was Class 3's penny line?*

2. Write a number story using the following information.

   (a) | 5 km | five times as far |

   (b) | 8 chocolate bars | 4 times as many |

   _____

   _____

   _____

   _____

   _____

   _____

CHALLENGE On a piece of paper, write two word problems for a friend to solve.

Objective *Solves positive integer scaling multiplication problems.*

TEACHER INFORMATION

MULTIPLICATION AND DIVISION

Objective

- Solve problems involving multiplication, including correspondence problems in which n objects are connected to m objects.

Oral work and mental calculation

- Use the appropriate vocabulary: *operation*, *sign*, *symbol*, *number sentence* and *equation*.

- Give the class a word problem. Ask them whether it needs addition, subtraction, multiplication or division to solve the word problem. Discuss how they know.

- Work out the answer to the word problem. Discuss how to best work it out. Can it be worked out mentally or do they need to work it out on paper? Do the pupils need apparatus to help work it out; for example, a number line, cubes or coins?

- Give pupils a simple multiplication statement; for example, 6 x 5. Ask pupils to make up a word problem that reflects this multiplication statement.

Main teaching activity

Multiplication word problems (page 113)

Additional activities suitable for developing the objective

- Work out word problems and write the answer in a number sentence; for example,

  An apple costs 25p. How much will six apples cost?

- Give pupils a simple multiplication statement; for example, 5 x 3. Ask pupils to write a word problem that reflects this multiplication statement.

- Write the unknown operation sign into number sentences; for example, 9 ? 5 = 45.

Answers

1. (a) 5 x 3 = 15   (b) 7 x 2 = 14
   (c) 4 x 10 = 40   (d) 3 x 9 = 27
   (e) 48 x 2 = 96   (f) 12 x 5 = 60
   (g) 65 x 3 = 195   (h) 70 x 4 = 280

2. (a) 3 x 6 = 18, Teacher check
   (b) 32 x 4 = 128, Teacher check

Challenge: Teacher check

MULTIPLICATION WORD PROBLEMS

1. Read, set out and solve these multiplication word problems.

(a) 5 children each have 3 dolls. How many dolls altogether?	$5 \times 3 =$ _____	(b) 7 children each have 2 basketballs. How many basketballs altogether?	
(c) 4 vases each contain 10 tulips. How many tulips altogether?		(d) 3 bookshelves each hold 9 books. How many books altogether?	
(e) 2 buses are heading to the city, each holding 48 passengers. How many passengers altogether?	$\begin{array}{r} 48 \\ \times\ 2 \\ \hline \\ \hline \end{array}$	(f) 5 packets of biscuits each contain 12 biscuits. How many biscuits altogether?	
(g) 3 aeroplanes each carry 65 passengers overseas. How many passengers altogether?		(h) 4 packets of lollipops each contain 70 lollipops. How many lollipops altogether?	

2. Write your own multiplication word problems for the following.

(a) 3 x 6 = _____

(b) 32 x 4 = _____

CHALLENGE Check your answers. Tick (✔) them if they are correct and cross (✗) them if they are incorrect. Redo the incorrect sums on the back of the sheet.

Objective   *Selects appropriate methods to solve word problems involving multiplication of whole numbers.*

TEACHER INFORMATION

MULTIPLICATION AND DIVISION

Objective

- Solve problems involving division, including correspondence problems in which n objects are connected to m objects.

Oral work and mental calculation

- Use the appropriate vocabulary: operation, sign, symbol, number sentence and equation.

- Give the class a word problem. Ask them whether it needs addition, subtraction, multiplication or division to solve the word problem. Discuss how they know.

- Work out the answer to the word problem. Discuss how to best work it out. Can it be worked out mentally or do they need to work it out on paper? Do the pupils need apparatus to help work it out; for example, a number line, cubes or coins?

- Give pupils a simple division statement; for example, 25 ÷ 5. Ask pupils to make up a word problem that reflects this division statement.

Main teaching activity

Division word problems (page 115)

Additional activities suitable for developing the objective

- Work out word problems and write the answer in a number sentence; for example,

  Jamil has 35 fairy cakes. He shares them between seven friends. How many cakes does each friend have?

- Give pupils a simple division statement; for example, 20 ÷ 4. Ask pupils to write a word problem that reflects this division statement.

- Write the unknown operation sign into number sentences; for example, 12 ? 3 = 4.

Answers

1. (a) 15 ÷ 3 = 5   (b) 20 ÷ 5 = 4
   (c) 18 ÷ 3 = 6   (d) 24 ÷ 2 = 12
   (e) 21 ÷ 3 = 7   (f) 16 ÷ 4 = 4
   (g) 12 ÷ 3 = 4   (h) 27 ÷ 5 = 5 r 2

2. (a) 14 ÷ 2 = 7, Teacher check
   (b) 18 ÷ 4 = 4 r 2, Teacher check

Challenge: Teacher check

DIVISION WORD PROBLEMS

1. Read, set out and solve these division word problems.

(a) 15 pencils shared among 3 children. How many pencils each?	$15 \div 3 =$ _____	(b) 20 apples were shared among 5 horses. How many did each horse get?	
(c) 18 books shared among 3 shelves. How many on each shelf?		(d) 24 sweets shared between 2 children. How many sweets each?	
(e) 21 stickers shared among 3 children. How many stickers each?		(f) 16 biscuits shared among 4 boys. How many biscuits each?	
(g) 12 slices of pizza shared among 3 people. How many slices of pizza each?		(h) 27 people travel in 5 cars. How many in each car? Any remainders?	

2. Write your own division word problems for the following.

(a) $14 \div 2 =$ _____

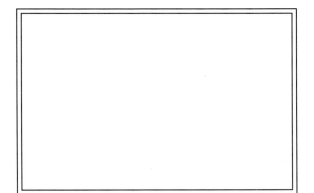

(b) $18 \div 4 =$ _____

CHALLENGE Check your answers. Tick (✔) them if they are correct and cross (✗) them if they are incorrect. Redo the incorrect sums on the back of the sheet.

Objective   *Selects appropriate methods to solve word problems involving division of whole numbers.*

TEACHER INFORMATION

MULTIPLICATION AND DIVISION

Objective

- Solve problems involving multiplication and division, including positive integer scaling problems and correspondence problems in which n objects are connected to m objects.

Oral work and mental calculation

- Use and understand the vocabulary *operation, sign, symbol, number sentence.*

- Take a simple calculation and, as a class, decide what would be the best method to use to work it out. Can we do it in our heads? Do we need to use a pencil and paper? Do we need apparatus such as counters or cubes?

- Take a simple word problem and, as a class, decide which operation is needed to solve it.

- Practise checking solutions to problems by rereading the problem to ensure the solution looks correct and using checking strategies; for example, checking with an equivalent calculation or completing addition and multiplication in a different order.

Main teaching activity

Matching number stories (page 117)

Additional activities suitable for developing the objective

- Make up some number stories to reflect statements; for example,

  $\triangle \times 2 = 18$ $20 \div \triangle = 5$

- Fill in missing signs in sums; for example, $5 \triangle 2 = 10$.

- Write number sentences in response to number stories; for example, Suzanne has 9 stickers and Sunita has twice as many. They have 27 stickers altogether.

Answers

1. (a) frogs – $2 \times 4 = 8$
   (b) biscuits – $7 \times 3 = 21$
   (c) pencils – $18 \div 2 = 9$
   (d) stickers – $20 \div 4 = 5$
   (e) budgies – $12 \times 2 = 24$
   (f) money – $8p \times 4 = 32p$

Challenge: Teacher check

MATCHING NUMBER STORIES

1. Match the number story with the picture to the number sentence.

Number story	Picture	Number sentence
(a) There are 2 logs in the pond with 4 frogs sitting on each. How many frogs are there altogether?	• •	8p x 4 32p
(b) Luke has 7 biscuits in his jar. Laura has 3 times as many. How many biscuits has Laura?	• •	2 x 4 = 8
(c) John has 18 pencils. Jamie has half as many. How many pencils has Jamie?	• •	7 x 3 = 21
(d) 20 stickers are shared out among 4 children. How many stickers does each child get?	• •	18 ÷ 2 = 9
(e) Karen had 12 budgies. Each had a baby. How many budgies does Karen have now?	• •	20 ÷ 4 = 5
(f) Emily has 8p. Jack has 4 times more. How much money does Jack have?	• •	12 x 2 = 24

CHALLENGE

Check your answers and tick below to show whether you think you are correct.

(a) ☐   (b) ☐   (c) ☐   (d) ☐   (e) ☐   (f) ☐

Objective *Matches a number story with its answer.*

TEACHER INFORMATION

FRACTIONS

Objectives

- Count up and down in tenths; recognise that tenths arise from dividing an object into 10 equal parts and in dividing one-digit numbers or quantities by 10.

- Solve problems that involve the above.

Oral work and mental calculation

- Count on and back, as a class, in tenths.

- Arrange tenths on a number line.

- Use a number line, marked in tenths, to respond to questions; for example,

  Count on $^3/_{10}$ from $^6/_{10}$.

  Count back $^5/_{10}$ from $^8/_{10}$.

- Build a tower using 10 Unifix cubes. Discuss the different colours used; for example, $^3/_{10}$ is red, $^4/_{10}$ is blue.

Main teaching activity

Tenths (page 119)

Additional activities suitable for developing the objectives

- Complete number sequences; for example,

  $^3/_{10}$, $^4/_{10}$ —, —, $^7/_{10}$.

- Arrange tenths, written onto cards, in order from smallest to largest, and vice versa.

- Build a tower using 10 Unifix cubes. Make a coloured drawing of the tower and label the fraction of each colour.

- Provide pupils with drawings of shapes split into 10 equal parts. Ask them to colour different fractions of the shapes. Convert to decimals.

Answers

1. $^2/_{10}$, $^4/_{10}$, $^7/_{10}$, $^8/_{10}$

2. Teacher check

3. (a) $^4/_{10}$ (b) $^9/_{10}$ (c) $^7/_{10}$

4. Teacher check

5. (a) $^8/_{10}$ (b) $^3/_{10}$ (c) $^5/_{10}$

Challenge: (a) $^2/_{10}$, $^4/_{10}$, $^8/_{10}$, $^9/_{10}$

(b) $^1/_{10}$, $^4/_{10}$, $^5/_{10}$, $^8/_{10}$

TENTHS

1. Fill in the missing tenths on the number line.

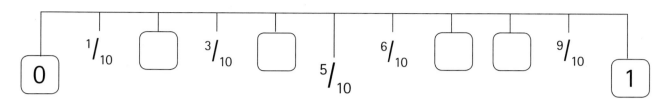

2. Shade the following tenths in the shapes.

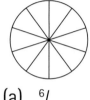

(a) $^6/_{10}$

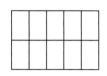

(b) $^3/_{10}$

(c) $^8/_{10}$

3. Write how many tenths have been shaded on the following shapes.

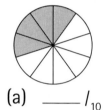

(a) ——— $/_{10}$

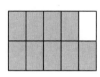

(b) ——— $/_{10}$

(c) ——— $/_{10}$

4. Shade the following tenths in the groups of objects.

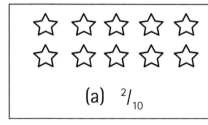

(a) $^2/_{10}$

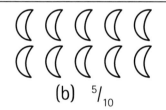

(b) $^5/_{10}$

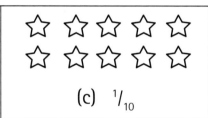

(c) $^1/_{10}$

5. Write how many tenths have been shaded in the groups of objects.

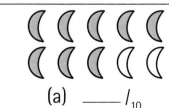

(a) ——— $/_{10}$

(b) ——— $/_{10}$

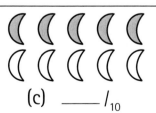

(c) ——— $/_{10}$

CHALLENGE (a) Write the number that is one tenth **more** than these fractions.

$^1/_{10}$, ——— $/_{10}$ $^3/_{10}$, ——— $/_{10}$ $^7/_{10}$, ——— $/_{10}$ $^8/_{10}$, ——— $/_{10}$

(b) Write the number that is one tenth **less** than these fractions.

$^2/_{10}$, ——— $/_{10}$ $^5/_{10}$, ——— $/_{10}$ $^6/_{10}$, ——— $/_{10}$ $^9/_{10}$, ——— $/_{10}$

Objective *Recognises and counts in tenths.*

TEACHER INFORMATION

FRACTIONS

Objectives

- Recognise, find and write fractions of a discrete set of objects: unit fractions and non-unit fractions with small denominators.

- Solve problems that involve the above.

Oral work and mental calculation

- Use the vocabulary: *fraction, half, third, quarter, fifth, sixth, seventh, eighth, ninth, tenth, whole, denominator, numerator.*

- Display four coloured balls. Discuss the fraction that is red, blue, green or yellow. Write the fraction on the board. Repeat with 5/6/7/8/9/10 coloured balls.

- Cut a cake or piece of fruit into quarters. Give pupils different fractions; for example, give Jane $^1/_4$ and Kellis $^3/_4$. Discuss which is the larger fraction. Cut the cake or piece of fruit again, into eighths. Give pupils different fractions and discuss.

Main teaching activity

Fractions (page 121)

Additional activities suitable for developing the objectives

- Divide a square into quarters. Shade $^1/_4$ with red stripes, $^2/_4$ with blue dots, $^3/_4$ with yellow waves and $^4/_4$ with green stars. Discuss.

- Repeat with other shapes and fractions.

Answers

1. (a) two, $^2/_3$ (b) one, $^1/_4$ (c) one, $^1/_2$
   (d) five, $^5/_6$ (e) one, $^1/_8$ (f) five, $^5/_9$
   (g) one, $^1/_1$ (h) three, $^3/_5$

2. (a) three, $^3/_4$ (b) one, $^1/_2$ (c) three, $^3/_6$
   (d) one, $^1/_3$ (e) seven, $^7/_{10}$ (f) two, $^2/_5$
   (g) three, $^3/_7$ (h) three, $^3/_9$

Challenge: Teacher check

FRACTIONS

The number at the bottom of a fraction (*denominator*) tells us how many parts the whole is divided into. The number at the top (*numerator*) tells us how many parts are shaded.

For example; for $^3/_4$, the shape is divided into 4 parts and 3 parts are shaded.

1. Write the fraction that is shaded.

(a)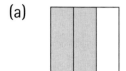

_____ thirds $/_3$

(b)

_____ quarter $/_4$

(c)

_____ half $/_2$

(d)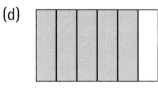

_____ sixths $/_6$

(e)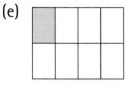

_____ eighth $/_8$

(f)

_____ ninths $/_9$

(g)

_____ whole $/_1$

(h)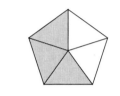

_____ fifths $/_5$

2. Write the fraction that is shaded.

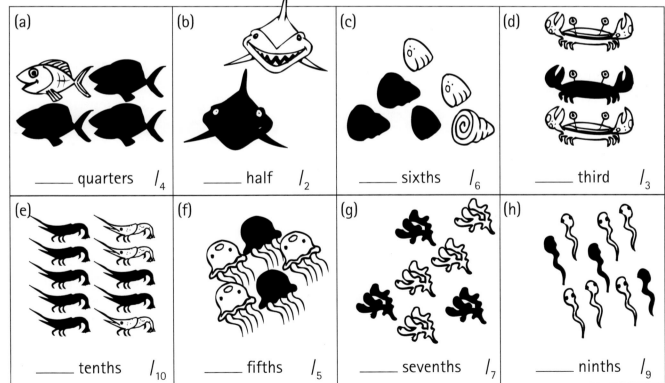

(a)

_____ quarters $/_4$

(b)

_____ half $/_2$

(c)

_____ sixths $/_6$

(d)

_____ third $/_3$

(e)

_____ tenths $/_{10}$

(f)

_____ fifths $/_5$

(g)

_____ sevenths $/_7$

(h)

_____ ninths $/_9$

CHALLENGE Count how many pupils are in your class and write the number
_____. What fraction of that number have brown hair? _____
black hair? _____ blonde hair? _____ red hair? _____

Objective *Identifies and represents fractional parts of collections or objects.*

TEACHER INFORMATION

FRACTIONS

Objectives

- Recognise, find and write fractions of a discrete set of objects: unit fractions and non-unit fractions with small denominators.

- Recognise and use fractions as numbers: unit fractions and non-unit fractions with small denominators.

- Solve problems that involve the above.

Oral work and mental calculation

- Find half of each of the even numbers to 30. Answer questions such as: What is half of 14? Of 8? Of 18?

- Pupils stand in groups of eight. Ask $\frac{1}{2}$, $\frac{1}{4}$ or $\frac{3}{4}$ of the group to sit down.

- Ask pupils verbal questions; for example, What is $\frac{1}{5}$ of 10? What is $\frac{3}{4}$ of 20?

- Discuss the answers to word problems; for example,

  If 6 cakes are divided equally between 2 people, how many cakes would each person get?

Interactive whiteboard activity

Interactive whiteboard activity available to support this copymaster. Visit www.prim-ed.com.

Main teaching activity

Fractions of groups (page 123)

Additional activities suitable for developing the objectives

- Place 20 counters on a desk. Ring 2/4/5/10 of the counters with a string circle. Discuss what fraction is and is not in the ring.

- Each pupil has 10 cubes. They need to make a shape, which is; for example, $\frac{1}{2}$ red and $\frac{1}{10}$ blue.

- Work out the answers to word problems; for example,

  Melissa has 20p. She shares it equally between herself and 4 friends. How much money does each person have?

- Each pupil has 60 cubes. They need to work out what $\frac{1}{2}$, $\frac{1}{3}$, $\frac{1}{4}$, $\frac{1}{5}$ and $\frac{1}{10}$ of the 60 cubes is.

Answers

1. (a) 1   (b) 5   (c) 2   (d) 4

2. (a) 1   (b) 2   (c) 4   (d) 3

3. (a) 1   (b) 3   (c) 2   (d) 5

Challenge: Teacher check

FRACTIONS OF GROUPS

1. Shade $^1/_2$ of these groups and finish the number sentence.

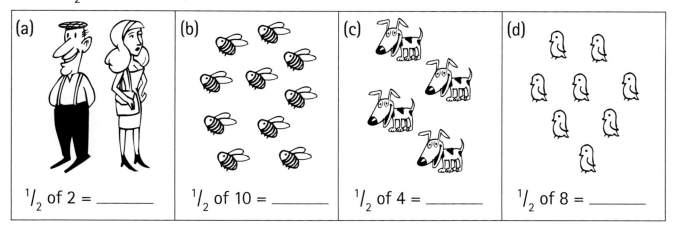

(a) $^1/_2$ of 2 = _____

(b) $^1/_2$ of 10 = _____

(c) $^1/_2$ of 4 = _____

(d) $^1/_2$ of 8 = _____

2. Shade $^1/_4$ of these groups and finish the number sentence.

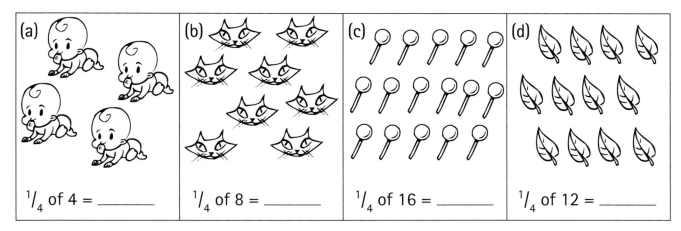

(a) $^1/_4$ of 4 = _____

(b) $^1/_4$ of 8 = _____

(c) $^1/_4$ of 16 = _____

(d) $^1/_4$ of 12 = _____

3. Shade $^1/_3$ of these groups and finish the number sentence.

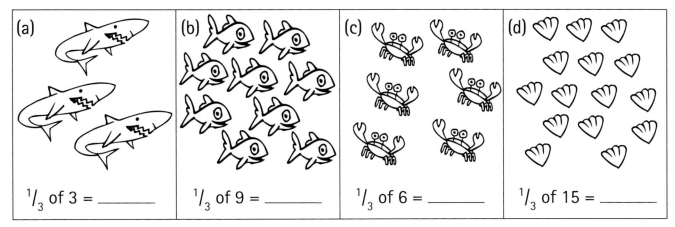

(a) $^1/_3$ of 3 = _____

(b) $^1/_3$ of 9 = _____

(c) $^1/_3$ of 6 = _____

(d) $^1/_3$ of 15 = _____

CHALLENGE Count how many children are in your class today.

If you had to divide the class in half,
how many children would be on each team? _____

If you had to divide the class into
quarters, how many would be on each team? _____

Objective   *Finds and records fractions of objects and numbers.*

TEACHER INFORMATION

FRACTIONS

Objectives

- Recognise and show, using diagrams, equivalent fractions with small denominators.
- Solve problems that involve the above.

Oral work and mental calculation

- Cut cakes/fruit into $\frac{1}{2}$, $\frac{2}{4}$, $\frac{5}{10}$ to show that although the fractions are different they are equivalent. Discuss.

- Hold up equivalent and non-equivalent fraction cards; for example, $\frac{1}{2}$ and $\frac{2}{4}$ or $\frac{2}{5}$ and $\frac{1}{3}$. Class says whether the two fractions are 'equivalent' or 'non-equivalent'.

Interactive whiteboard activity

Interactive whiteboard activity available to support this copymaster. Visit *www.prim-ed.com*.

Main teaching activity

Equivalent fractions (page 125)

Additional activities suitable for developing the objectives

- Give pupils a grid containing 10 squares. Tell them to shade in one half of the grid blue and then five tenths of the grid red. Discuss what they notice.

- Play 'Equivalent fractions bingo'. Call out the fraction and pupils have to cover an equivalent fraction on their bingo board with a counter.

- Each pupil has 20 cubes. Ask them to record what $\frac{1}{2}$, $\frac{1}{4}$, $\frac{2}{4}$, $\frac{3}{4}$, $\frac{1}{5}$, $\frac{2}{5}$, $\frac{3}{5}$, $\frac{4}{5}$, $\frac{5}{5}$, $\frac{1}{10}$, $\frac{2}{10}$, $\frac{3}{10}$, $\frac{4}{10}$, $\frac{5}{10}$, $\frac{6}{10}$, $\frac{7}{10}$, $\frac{8}{10}$, $\frac{9}{10}$ and $\frac{10}{10}$ of the cubes are. Are any of the answers the same? Investigate whether these fractions are therefore equivalent.

Answers

1. Teacher check

2. (a) $\frac{2}{2}$ (b) $\frac{2}{10}$ (c) $\frac{2}{4}$ (d) $\frac{2}{5}$
   (e) $\frac{8}{10}$ (f) $\frac{5}{10}$ (g) $\frac{1}{2}$, $\frac{2}{4}$ (h) 1 whole

3. (a) ✔   (b) ✗   (c) ✔   (d) ✗

Challenge: Teacher check, yes

EQUIVALENT FRACTIONS

1. The chart below shows how some fractions can be equivalent (the same).
   Colour each fraction line a different colour.

whole $\frac{1}{1}$								
half				$\frac{1}{2}$				
third		$\frac{1}{3}$			$\frac{1}{3}$			
quarter		$\frac{1}{4}$		$\frac{1}{4}$			$\frac{1}{4}$	
fifth	$\frac{1}{5}$		$\frac{1}{5}$		$\frac{1}{5}$			$\frac{1}{5}$	
tenth	$\frac{1}{10}$	$\frac{1}{10}$	$\frac{1}{10}$	$\frac{1}{10}$	$\frac{1}{10}$	$\frac{1}{10}$	$\frac{1}{10}$	$\frac{1}{10}$

2. Use the equivalence chart above to help you answer these questions.

(a) 1 whole = $/_2$

(b) $\frac{1}{5} = /_{10}$

(c) $\frac{1}{2} = /_4$

(d) $^4/_{10} = /_5$

(e) $^4/_5 = /_{10}$

(f) $\frac{1}{2} = /_{10}$

(g) $^5/_{10} = /_2$ and $/_4$

(h) $^2/_2, \, ^3/_3, \, ^4/_4, \, ^5/_5, \, ^{10}/_{10} =$ _____

3. Tick (✔) the fractions that are equivalent and cross (✗) the fractions that are not.

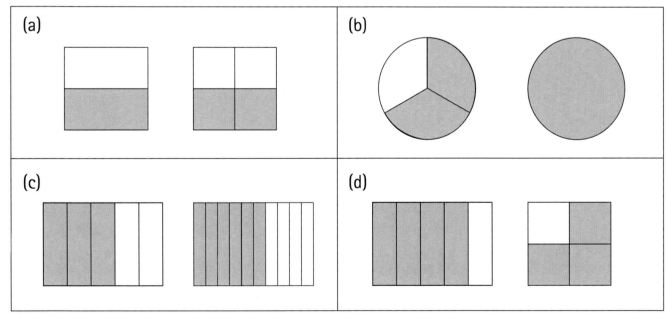

CHALLENGE

On the back of this sheet, trace two circles. Divide the first into quarters and shade $^2/_4$, divide the second into halves and shade in $\frac{1}{2}$. Are these fractions equivalent? [yes] [no]

Objective   *Identifies equivalent fractions with small denominators.*

TEACHER INFORMATION

FRACTIONS

Objectives

- Add fractions with the same denominator within one whole.

- Solve problems that involve the above.

Oral work and mental calculation

- Hold up cards showing two fractions with the same denominator. Mentally add them. (Keep answers to within one whole).

- Mentally solve word problems involving the addition of fractions; for example,

  The twins had 12 football stickers. Kasim stuck $^5/_{12}$ of the stickers in his album and so did Kara. How many stickers got stuck into their albums?

Main teaching activity

Adding fractions (page 127)

Additional activities suitable for developing the objectives

- Complete shape and number fraction addition sums, like the ones in Questions 1 and 2.

- Solve word problems involving the addition of fractions; for example,

  The pizza had 8 slices. Dad ate $^3/_8$ and so did Mum. How many slices did they eat altogether?

Answers

1. (a) $^3/_4$ (b) $^2/_3$ (c) $^3/_5$ (d) $^6/_8$
   (e) $^5/_6$ (f) $^9/_{10}$

2. (a) $^3/_4$ (b) $^3/_5$ (c) $^5/_6$ (d) $^6/_7$
   (e) $^7/_8$ (f) $^7/_9$ (g) $^9/_{10}$ (h) $^{10}/_{12}$
   (i) $^{15}/_{20}$ (j) $^6/_8$ (k) $^6/_9$ (l) $^9/_{10}$
   (m) $^{10}/_{12}$ (n) $^{13}/_{15}$ (o) $^{19}/_{20}$

Challenge: Jemima = 2, Jude = 5, Jeremiah = 3
Total = 10 apples

ADDING FRACTIONS

1. Use the shapes to help add the fractions.

(a) 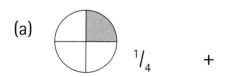 $^1/_4$ + $^2/_4$ = ___ $/_4$

(b) 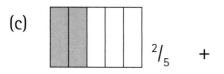 $^1/_3$ + $^1/_3$ = ___ $/_3$

(c) $^2/_5$ + $^1/_5$ = ___ $/_5$

(d) $^4/_8$ + $^2/_8$ = ___ $/_8$

(e) $^3/_6$ + $^2/_6$ = ___ $/_6$

(f) $^7/_{10}$ + $^2/_{10}$ = ___ $/_{10}$

2. Complete the fraction addition sums.

(a) $^2/_4 + ^1/_4 =$ ___ $/$ ___

(b) $^1/_5 + ^2/_5 =$ ___ $/$ ___

(c) $^4/_6 + ^1/_6 =$ ___ $/$ ___

(d) $^3/_7 + ^3/_7 =$ ___ $/$ ___

(e) $^5/_8 + ^2/_8 =$ ___ $/$ ___

(f) $^3/_9 + ^4/_9 =$ ___ $/$ ___

(g) $^6/_{10} + ^3/_{10} =$ ___ $/$ ___

(h) $^6/_{12} + ^4/_{12} =$ ___ $/$ ___

(i) $^{10}/_{20} + ^5/_{20} =$ ___ $/$ ___

(j) $^2/_8 + ^3/_8 + ^1/_8 =$ ___ $/$ ___

(k) $^3/_9 + ^1/_9 + ^2/_9 =$ ___ $/$ ___

(l) $^5/_{10} + ^2/_{10} + ^2/_{10} =$ ___ $/$ ___

(m) $^7/_{12} + ^2/_{12} + ^1/_{12} =$ ___ $/$ ___

(n) $^5/_{15} + ^6/_{15} + ^2/_{15} =$ ___ $/$ ___

(o) $^{12}/_{20} + ^2/_{20} + ^5/_{20} =$ ___ $/$ ___

CHALLENGE

There are 12 apples in the bowl. Jemima eats $^2/_{12}$, Jude eats $^5/_{12}$ and Jeremiah eats $^3/_{12}$.

How many apples does each person eat? Jemima = ___, Jude = ___, Jeremiah = ___

How many apples are eaten altogether? ___ apples

Objective   *Adds fractions with the same denominator.*

TEACHER INFORMATION

FRACTIONS

Objectives

- Subtract fractions with the same denominator within one whole.

- Solve problems that involve the above.

Oral work and mental calculation

- Hold up cards showing two fractions with the same denominator. Mentally subtract them. (Keep within one whole).

- Mentally solve word problems involving the subtraction of fractions; for example,

  Abdul had 10 football stickers. He gave $^2/_{10}$ of his stickers to James and $^3/_{10}$ to Mandy. How many stickers did he have left?

Main teaching activity

Subtracting fractions (page 129)

Additional activities suitable for developing the objectives

- Complete shape and number fraction subtraction sums, like the ones in Questions 1 and 2.

- Solve word problems involving the subtraction of fractions; for example,

  The pizza had 8 slices. Dad ate $^3/_8$ and Mum ate $^2/_8$. How many slices were left?

Answers

1. (a) $^1/_4$ (b) $^1/_3$ (c) $^2/_5$ (d) $^1/_8$
   (e) $^2/_6$ (f) $^2/_{10}$

2. (a) $^2/_4$ (b) $^3/_5$ (c) $^2/_6$ (d) $^4/_7$
   (e) $^3/_8$ (f) $^1/_9$ (g) $^4/_{10}$ (h) $^9/_{12}$
   (i) $^{14}/_{20}$ (j) $^2/_8$ (k) $^1/_9$ (l) $^3/_{10}$
   (m) $^1/_{12}$ (n) $^4/_{15}$ (o) $^1/_{20}$

Challenge: Chris = 4, Cate = 5, Caleb = 6
            Cookies left = 5

SUBTRACTING FRACTIONS

1. Use the shapes to help subtract the fractions.

(a) 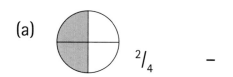 $^2/_4$ – $^1/_4$ = ___ $/_4$

(b) $^2/_3$ – $^1/_3$ = ___ $/_3$

(c) $^4/_5$ – $^2/_5$ = ___ $/_5$

(d) 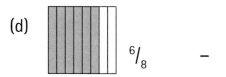 $^6/_8$ – 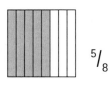 $^5/_8$ =  ___ $/_8$

(e) 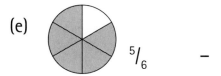 $^5/_6$ – 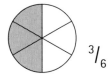 $^3/_6$ =  ___ $/_6$

(f) 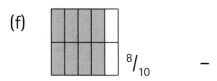 $^8/_{10}$ – 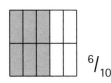 $^6/_{10}$ = ___ $/_{10}$

2. Complete the fraction subtraction sums.

(a) $^3/_4 - ^1/_4 =$ ___ / ___   (b) $^4/_5 - ^1/_5 =$ ___ / ___   (c) $^5/_6 - ^3/_6 =$ ___ / ___

(d) $^6/_7 - ^2/_7 =$ ___ / ___   (e) $^6/_8 - ^3/_8 =$ ___ / ___   (f) $^7/_9 - ^6/_9 =$ ___ / ___

(g) $^9/_{10} - ^5/_{10} =$ ___ / ___   (h) $^{11}/_{12} - ^2/_{12} =$ ___ / ___   (i) $^{17}/_{20} - ^3/_{20} =$ ___ / ___

(j) $^7/_8 - ^2/_8 - ^3/_8 =$ ___ / ___   (k) $^8/_9 - ^1/_9 - ^6/_9 =$ ___ / ___

(l) $^9/_{10} - ^2/_{10} - ^4/_{10} =$ ___ / ___   (m) $^{10}/_{12} - ^3/_{12} - ^6/_{12} =$ ___ / ___

(n) $^{14}/_{15} - ^2/_{15} - ^8/_{15} =$ ___ / ___   (o) $^{18}/_{20} - ^{15}/_{20} - ^2/_{20} =$ ___ / ___

CHALLENGE

There are 20 cookies in the cookie jar. Chris eats $^4/_{20}$ cookies, Cate eats $^5/_{20}$ and Caleb eats $^6/_{20}$. How many cookies does each person eat? Chris = ___, Cate = ___, Caleb = ___

How many cookies are left? ___ cookies

Objective   *Subtracts fractions with the same denominator.*

TEACHER INFORMATION

FRACTIONS

Objectives

- Compare and order unit fractions, and fractions with the same denominator.

- Solve problems that involve the above.

Oral work and mental calculation

- Place fractions, in order of size, on the class washing line. Answer questions; for example, What fraction lies exactly between $^1/_4$ and $^3/_4$?

- Show the pupils jars with varying amounts of water in them. Ask them to point to the jar that is $^1/_2$, $^1/_4$, $^3/_4$, $^1/_{10}$ etc. full. Then order the jars by the amount of water that they contain.

Interactive whiteboard activity

Interactive whiteboard activity available to support this copymaster. Visit *www.prim-ed.com.*

Main teaching activity

Comparing and ordering fractions - 1 (page 131)

Additional activities suitable for developing the objectives

- Fill glass jars or bottles with varying fractions of water. Order the jars by the amount of water that they contain, from smallest to largest.

- Make fraction number lines. Answer true/false questions; for example,

  $^2/_4$ is greater than $^3/_4$ – true or false?

  $^2/_3$ is between $^1/_3$ and 1 – true or false?

- Sort a selection of fractions written onto cards according to whether they are greater than or less than one half/one quarter.

- Write a selection of given fractions from smallest to largest, and vice versa.

Answers

1. (a) $^1/_2$ (b) $^3/_4$ (c) $^5/_{10}$

2. (a) $^1/_2$ (b) $^1/_2$ (c) $^3/_{10}$

3. (a) $^2/_4$ or $^1/_2$ (b) $^8/_{10}$ or $^4/_5$ (c) $^2/_5$, $^4/_5$
   (d) $^2/_8$, $^4/_8$, $^6/_8$

Challenge: (a) False   (b) True   (c) True   (d) True
(e) False   (f) True

COMPARING AND ORDERING FRACTIONS - 1

1. Tick the larger fraction in each pair.

(a)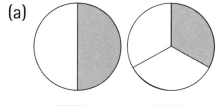

$^1/_2$ ☐ $^1/_3$ ☐

(b)

$^1/_4$ ☐ $^3/_4$ ☐

(c)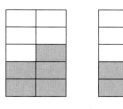

$^5/_{10}$ ☐ $^2/_5$ ☐

2. Tick the smaller fraction in each pair.

(a)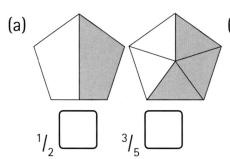

$^1/_2$ ☐ $^3/_5$ ☐

(b)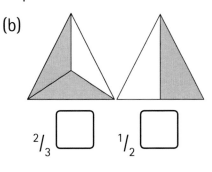

$^2/_3$ ☐ $^1/_2$ ☐

(c)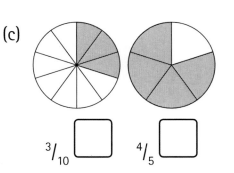

$^3/_{10}$ ☐ $^4/_5$ ☐

3. Fill in the missing fractions on the number lines.

(a)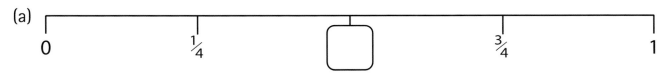

(b)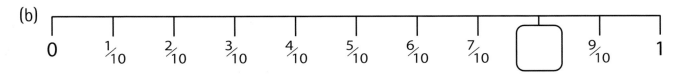

(c)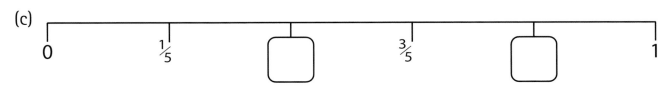

(d)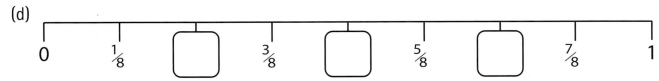

CHALLENGE

Circle **True** or **False**.

(a) $^2/_4 > ^3/_4$ True/False   (b) $^4/_5 > ^1/_5$ True/False   (c) $^6/_8 > ^1/_8$ True/False

(d) $^3/_6 < ^4/_6$ True/False   (e) $^1/_3 > ^2/_3$ True/False   (f) $^7/_{10} > ^2/_{10}$ True/False

Objective   *Compares and orders fractions.*

TEACHER INFORMATION

FRACTIONS

Objectives

- Compare and order unit fractions, and fractions with the same denominator.
- Solve problems that involve the above.

Oral work and mental calculation

- Place fractions, in order of size, on the class washing line. Answer questions; for example, What fraction lies exactly between $\frac{1}{4}$ and $\frac{3}{4}$?
- Show the pupils jars with varying amounts of water in them. Ask them to point to the jar that is $\frac{1}{2}$, $\frac{1}{4}$, $\frac{3}{4}$, $\frac{1}{10}$ etc. full. Then order the jars by the amount of water that they contain.

Main teaching activity

Comparing and ordering fractions - 2 (page 133)

Additional activities suitable for developing the objectives

- Fill glass jars or bottles with varying fractions of water. Order the jars by the amount of water that they contain, from smallest to largest.
- Make fraction number lines. Answer true/false questions; for example,

  $\frac{2}{4}$ is greater than $\frac{3}{4}$ – true or false?

  $\frac{2}{3}$ is between $\frac{1}{3}$ and 1 – true or false?

- Sort a selection of fractions written onto cards according to whether they are greater than or less than one half/one quarter.
- Write a selection of given fractions from smallest to largest, and vice versa.

Answers

1. 2, 1, 5, 3, 4

2. Teacher check

3. (b) $\frac{2}{4}$, $\frac{3}{4}$ (c) $\frac{2}{6}$, $\frac{4}{6}$, $\frac{5}{6}$
   (d) $\frac{1}{8}$, $\frac{3}{8}$, $\frac{4}{8}$, $\frac{5}{8}$, $\frac{7}{8}$, $\frac{8}{8}$

Challenge: (a) 2, 3, 4 (b) 2 (c) 3

COMPARING AND ORDERING FRACTIONS - 2

1. Number the fractions 1 to 5 from the smallest to the largest.

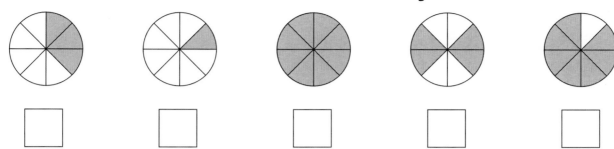

2. Colour the fractions that look the same size in the same colour.

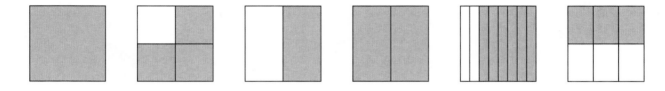

3. Number lines can show us how different fractions can be the same size. Fill in the missing fractions on the number lines.

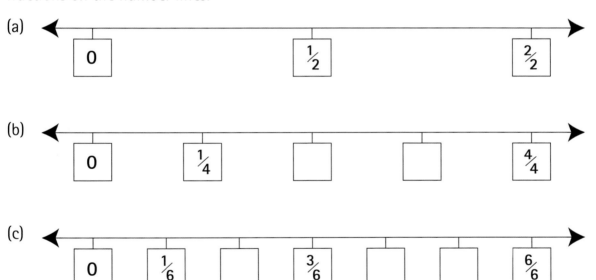

CHALLENGE

Using the number lines above, fill in these fraction statements.

(a) $^1/_2 =$ ____$/_4 =$ ____$/_6 =$ ____$/_8$ (b) $^1/_4 =$ ____$/_8$ (c) $^6/_8 =$ ____$/_4$

Objective   *Compares and orders fractional parts of objects.*